W9-BXX-878

What Preview Readers Have To Say

"The communities we live in expect us to turn to one another and say that things are great, kids are great...love my job. But, are we really doing 'great'? This little story really drills down into that facade we so readily put up for others to admire. Wherever you are in life—young, old, affluent, struggling to make ends meet—the nagging questions of life have to be dealt with. I think *THE BREAKTHROUGH* pushes one to rethink the way most of us are living our lives. Perhaps one of the more important 'pushes' that you can receive."

—**LOUIS GIULIANO,** Former Chairman, President, and CEO of ITT Corp.

"With the recent financial collapse, many in the marketplace are hurting. Promotions are gone, bonuses are gone...many are searching for something more...something everlasting. Prepare yourself to be introduced to a new and better way of living! No matter how skeptical you may be, I urge you to approach *THE BREAKTHROUGH* with an open mind. You just might discover the secrets to everlasting peace, joy, and happiness."

—**MARK LINSZ**, Corporate Treasurer, Bank of America

"How we view the world and live our lives has a huge impact not only on us, but also on our loved ones, our communities, and even our culture. *THE BREAKTHROUGH* is a powerful parable and presents an excellent opportunity for people to consider whether there might be a better way of understanding life. As a follow up, I encourage every reader to attend an Alpha course to find out how it is that millions of lives are being transformed around the world."

—**CHUCK COLSON,** Founder, The Chuck Colson Center for Christian Worldview; Founder, Prison Fellowship

"Gerard Long's *THE BREAKTHROUGH* helps to give purpose, meaning, and understanding to life's biggest questions. Long writes in an honest, straight-forward fashion—helping one see the pathway to getting the most out of life. His Dr. David Heeley felt—like so many of us—that he had all the answers to life's questions until his children and Alpha helped him realize that he wasn't even asking the right questions. *THE BREAKTHROUGH* is a compelling read."

—**BOB MILLIGAN,** Founder and Chairman, M.I. Industries and Nature's Variety Inc.; Immediate Past Chairman, U. S. Chamber of Commerce

"Gerard Long has written a wonderful book that will appeal to Christians and non-Christians alike. The Alpha course has been successful worldwide and has appeal to churches of varying denominations. This book will be of great interest to all, as it addresses important questions all of us must confront in our lives."

—**PHILIP F. ANSCHUTZ**, Chairman and CEO, The Anschutz Corporation, parent company of Walden Media, which produced *The Chronicles of Narnia: The Lion, the Witch and the Wardrobe.*

"Each of us has her own life journey and what others see sometimes looks very different from what it really is. Secretly, we wonder, 'Does my life have purpose? Do my children, my husband, my work, my reputation fill me up?' Read *THE BREAKTHROUGH* and then begin the Alpha course journey to confront the inner longings which keep us striving for those things that fade away rather than those things that last eternally."

—**JACKIE J. RENWICK,** Founder and President, The Mustard Seed, A Fair Trade Shop Inc.

THE BREAKTHROUGH

THE BREAKTHROUGH

GERARD LONG

What If You Could Discover Life's Most Meaningful Answers in Today's Incredibly Uncertain World?

Published in North America by Alpha North America, 2275 Half Day Road, Suite 185, Deerfield, IL 60015

Printed in the USA.

10 11 12 13 14 15 16 17 / 10 9 8 7 6 5 4 3 2 1

DEDICATION

To Alex.
Remembered always.
Loved by his family.
Beloved by his Everlasting Father.
May his last wish be granted…and his
parting prayer answered…
through the words and pages
of this book.

TABLE OF CONTENTS

FOREWORD

By Ken Blanchard, Ph.D.
Co-author of *The One Minute Manager*

With life constantly pressing in on us from all directions, only rarely do we have the time to pause to consider the big questions:

"What is my purpose in life?"

"What am I missing?"

And, perhaps the biggest question of all is, "What really happens when I die?"

My friend Gerard Long has had the opportunity to ponder these and other questions while walking through the valley of tragedy. Over the space of only a few months, his heart was broken into multiple pieces by the suicide of his 17-year-old son, the death of his sister, and the near death of his wife, caused by a broken heart as the result of the loss of her son.

How true it is that we see things differently through the lens of brokenness. Despite the pain, this can be a wonderful thing. Tragedy provides an opportunity for new life to spring forth.

Consider a forest fire. Initially, there appears to be utter devastation. But, over time, wonderful new life appears everywhere!

Even if you haven't faced any tragedies or any serious disappointments in your life, my hope is that, through the parable that follows, you might gain some new insights on the big questions of life. I hope that a ray of light from this story will help you break through to a fresh, exciting way of living.

There are three specific questions I urge you to consider as you read this parable. First, "Is there a dimension to life that I'm missing?" This question could open up all sorts of possibilities. I have witnessed the life that Gerard Long now enjoys, and he told me that one of his friends once said to him, "Gerard, you are seeing life in color, whereas I am only seeing it in black and white!" However good or bad you may feel your life is, could there be other possibilities worth exploring that could make it even better?

Second—and this question is truly significant—"Is there such a thing as eternal life?" To get the answer wrong could be a catastrophe. Of course, if you answer "yes," the next logical question is, "How do I ensure that I'm going to heaven?"

The third and final question I ask you to consider as you read THE BREAKTHROUGH is, "Could I be hurting one or more people by the way I'm living my life?" This could also have huge consequences. What if I have a number of blind spots in my life, and my words, actions, and attitudes have hurt or are hurting other people? Just imagine the good that would result if, instead of causing pain, I became a channel of blessing.

There is a concept in science called the "butterfly effect." The idea is that everything in existence is interrelated—a butterfly flapping its wings in the Amazon in Brazil could set off a tornado in Texas! If you apply this concept to our relationships, it means that whomever I'm living for and how I'm living my life *is* having an impact on other people—whether I recognize it or not!

There is one other important suggestion I have for you. Please be open to the spiritual element within the parable. There are references to Jesus' teachings, and I'd love it if you would take a fresh look at these. I realize you may have had negative experiences with religion. In reality, many people share this complaint. You may have had contact with people who claim to be "Christians," but they say one thing and do another. Or they look down on other people and judge them in the process. By definition, they are not Christians—or at least they are not living as Christians.

The term Christian means "Christ follower," and Jesus did not judge, look down on, or disrespect people. On the contrary, he went out of his way to befriend the downtrodden and the marginalized people in society. He spoke against the hypocrisy of the religious system of the day. The latter, he taught, was a set of man's own rules, regulations, and traditions—and had nothing to do with the living God.

I hope that you enjoy the story and that you experience a breakthrough in your own life!

—**Ken Blanchard**
Escondido, CA, August, 2010

INTRODUCTION

If life were meant to be perfect, it would be. And it would be perfect in every way.

Everyone would be happy, healthy, and wealthy.

There would be no sickness, no accidents, no pain, no death.

There would be no strain in relationships, no divorce, no great divide between husbands and wives, between parents and children, or between management and staff.

There would be no form of racism or bigotry—and no war, crime, or prisons.

Of course, the obvious truth is that sickness, poverty, war, conflict, and death have proven themselves to be part of the human experience ever since we began keeping track of such things.

But this was not the way it was supposed to be. Life *was* meant to be perfect. Life was supposed to be a man and a woman—or men and women-—enjoying nature to its magnificent fullness, giving birth without pain, and living without end.

"That's absurd!" you exclaim. "How could that ever be?" you ask.

The answer is straightforward, yet mystifying. To discover

it, you will be asked to do something very challenging. You will be asked—while exploring the pages of this book—to "suspend your disbelief." To open your mind to the possibility that there is more than one kind of life. To understand and accept both the temporal and the eternal.

Are you up to the challenge? Are you an intellectually honest person? I sincerely hope you are.

The good news for you is that in the midst of all of life's problems—as inevitable as they are—you can experience a breakthrough. My goal in this book is to guide you along that exciting path! Please join me.

PROLOGUE

This is a story about imperfect people in an imperfect world, living their lives in imperfect ways.

If that sounds vaguely familiar, it could be because we might actually know these people. If we're really honest with ourselves, we might even admit that we *are* these people.

As you read the pages that follow, you may come to the conclusion that it must be my personal story that unfolds in this book. In a way, it is. In other ways, it isn't. That's because there are components of all of our stories that we hold in common. And there are other parts that are unique in our lives. I don't know about you, but I'm not about to include all the details of my life in a book!

But you need to know something up front about my point of view on life, on relationships, and on purpose and destiny. I believe that it's important to ask questions and be open to possible answers. And I believe the best answers to these questions are based on facts—on evidence.

There are probably a few people on earth who still believe that the earth is flat, or that the sun revolves around the earth. Of course, the evidence clearly tells us otherwise.

I also believe that, in this age of ever-expanding "grey areas," there are some "black and whites" that shouldn't be ignored. But how do we know what is black and what is white? The answer, I believe, is to ask honest questions and seek honest answers… then be open to those answers, even if they are in conflict with our long-held beliefs. Without that point of view, science never would have advanced. All of our great discoveries are the result of people who asked honest questions—not people who thought they already had all the answers.

I admit, though hesitantly, that I was once one of those people who thought he had all the answers. But some people came into my life who asked me a different set of questions, and that transformed my life!

In that spirit, this book asks more questions than it answers. Neither you nor I may ever find all the answers, but we certainly can focus on asking the right questions!

This book is about the promise of a wonderful life and an amazing future—despite the hardships and setbacks we may experience during the journey.

When you have finished reading, you will be asked to answer only four questions—"What do you, ***(Your Name Here)***, personally accept? What do you believe? What do you embrace?" And, "How will that make a difference in your life?"

ONE

A Perfect Life

David Heeley had always believed that he was nearly as perfect as any human being could possibly be. From the moment of his birth, his parents, Gilbert and Elaine, confirmed that viewpoint to their family and friends—always in David's presence. "David sleeps through the entire night. David never cries. David burps on command. David was nearly potty trained by eleven months of age. Imagine that!"

David began bringing home straight A's on his report card in first grade. That certainly would have been the case in kindergarten, too, but teachers didn't assign letter grades in kindergarten. In David's case, he was reading "chapter books" in first grade and doing fourth-grade math in third grade. And getting A's, of course.

In junior high school, David added music and athletics to his many achievements. He was a baseball natural, pitching and hitting his team to glory. He was "First Alternate" cellist in the All-State Orchestra by ninth grade. He'd hoped for first chair, but that wasn't quite meant to be.

High school graduation signaled the next in his line of successes. He was that year's salutatorian, second in a class of almost 600. This earned him offers of full-ride academic scholarships at two Ivy League schools, along with visits from four other NCAA college representatives who sought him for his baseball prowess.

His hard-working mom died when David was a sophomore at his university of choice, Cornell. It was the first life-shattering event in David's life. He had been very close to his mom. Mom was there for every practice, every game, every recital, every concert—even when his dad wasn't able to attend, for one reason or another. The pain of losing her was crushing. His dad had to take on a second job at an automotive parts factory, in addition to his full-time job as a long-haul truck driver, to make ends meet—and help David with room and board expenses so he could focus on his studies without the time-consuming pressure of a job.

Despite the mental and emotional setback of losing his mother, David graduated magna cum laude in biology from Cornell. He applied at several medical schools, and chose the Johns Hopkins School of Medicine at Johns Hopkins University in Baltimore—close enough to his home in Pennsylvania that his dad could pay him regular visits. Never mind the fact that "Perfect David Heeley" was accepted at what many consider to be the leading such institution in the world!

Today, the summer between Cornell and Johns Hopkins seems like a blur to David. But, back then, it was the most "real" time in his life.

During his summer back home with his dad, David reunited with his high school sweetheart, Elizabeth Dobransky. Their relationship in high school had its ups and downs, its twists and turns. In fact, to that point, dating Beth had been the only truly imperfect time in his life. At least that's the way he perceived it. David wanted sex. Beth didn't. "I want to be totally committed first," she explained, "and for me, that means marriage."

Initially, David thought Beth's refusal of his obvious advances were the unpleasant outcome of her "religious upbringing." Beth's entire family attended church every week. David's family had more "important" things to do.

Yet, David accepted her refusals with the somehow comforting thought that "there are lots of other fish in the sea. I'm sure, at Cornell, I'll meet some hot ladies who want to get caught!"

But this summer at home—the moment he saw her again—David knew the only fish he wanted to catch was Elizabeth Rachel Dobransky.

He tried again. His words glistened like the morning dew. His gentle touches instantly became her cherished memories. His soft kisses made her question her long-standing decision.

Still, Beth stood firm.

"Why?" David asked. "Is it me? Is there something about me you just don't like?"

Her response was more gratifying and satisfying than he ever imagined it could be.

"David, in my mind and in my heart, and even in my soul, there is a huge difference between love and sex. The man I marry is going to know—without any doubt—that I love him more than any other person on earth. He's going to know that I saved the best of me for the last man in my life. Things that no one else has ever experienced up to that point in time."

In his own way, David finally understood what she was saying. What he had always viewed as a purely physical act had seemingly become spiritual to her. So he accepted her wishes.

Despite the fact that they did not share the physical intimacy he had desired, their relationship was still filled with passion and tenderness. He would knock on her door on a rainy night, grab her by the hand, take her under his oversized umbrella, and lead her through animated conversations and huge, sloppy puddles in the street. He would kiss her every chance he got…and she gave him plenty of chances. He would touch her and caress her in every way she would allow.

It only made him want her more…love her more. The co-eds at Cornell easily and quickly drifted back into the dimly lit corners of his memory.

That summer, both David and Beth unexpectedly and passionately fell in love. Their affection and attention toward each other was unbridled. She became his "Honey Babe," and he became her "Stud Man."

At the end of the summer, two days before classes began at Johns Hopkins, they got married. There was no time for an official honeymoon. That would have to wait. For now, though, every day was a wonderful slice of honeymoon!

David had every reason to believe that his life was once again certain to march forward in a parade of perfection.

He graduated from Johns Hopkins in cardiology with highest honors and immediately connected with a group of investors—including his own frugal dad—who urged him to open his own practice.

Early in their marriage, David Heeley prided himself on his ability—and commitment—to be home for dinner with Beth every night.

It wasn't always easy during medical school. There were late classes, and even later opportunities to witness one-of-a-kind surgical procedures. It's difficult to say "no" when you're a part of emerging medical history. But his record was good: seven out of ten dinners together, on average.

At that time in her life, Beth felt as though her husband truly valued her. She knew she was appreciated. Although she never had the opportunity to attend even one day of college, she was intelligent and had "street smarts." She got a position as a sales rep for a beverage distribution company to help with expenses at home and at Johns Hopkins.

Her job was to make sure that the products she represented had good "shelf position" and as many "facings" as possible. In retail, this means that products should be placed at the "average adult eye level" (unless it's cereals or candy for kids—lower is better) and that more of her product should be visible to the shopper than the products of her competitors. Positioning, or placement, is both King and Queen.

Sometimes ideal positioning or placement requires that the rep has to show up at the store in the middle of the night—when fewer customers are around—to do "resets." This simply means the store management wants to put those products that are on sale, or are selling better, in the key position: at the right level with the right number of facings.

It was a tough job, and it took her away from her husband. But she knew she had to do it.

Time apart, though, especially in the formative years of a marriage, takes its toll. The changes in the relationship are subtle at first, but they eventually become increasingly noticeable.

Over not much time, Beth began to lose David's attention

and affection. And he began to lose the sparkle in his eyes, the compassion in his touch, and the passion in his kiss.

Over not much time, David had become more critical of his wife. His loving glances had become less frequent. His affirmative words had gone silent.

Feelings of isolation overcame her. Beth's heart ached for those gentle, loving touches she once received freely and frequently. She felt an increasing distance between herself and her career-driven husband. What was happening to the man she married?

Over not much time at all, life had become life. All of the stresses, challenges, and daily heartaches were becoming painfully obvious to both of them.

Then Beth became pregnant.

TWO

Babies Change Things

This fact is remarkably obvious to anyone who's ever had one. New babies are accompanied by massive change. Bedtime sex is replaced by feedings at 11:00 p.m., 1:00 a.m., 4:00 a.m.…or whenever the new bundle of blessing is ready and eager. Diapers and breast pumps are the new way of life. Erotic lingerie is gone for who-knows-however-long. So is a good night's sleep.

Beth knew this scenario was on her horizon the day her doctor said, "Good news! You're pregnant!" She was prepared for it. More than that, she was looking forward to it. Most parts of it, anyway. Secretly, she held onto thc hope that a baby would help fill the void that had swept over her marriage.

In direct contrast, David was clueless. The look on his face when she told him appeared to ask, "How could this happen?"

The months between the announcement and the birth seemed to crawl by, yet David was becoming increasingly comfortable with the idea of being a dad. Excited, even.

The delivery was difficult. After 22 hours of labor—and an

acutely increased heart rate on the part of the baby, the obstetrician concluded that a C-section was the optimal choice.

At 6:34 on a Tuesday night, Nichole Paige Heeley entered the world, took one look around, and cried.

In the most private recesses of his heart, David was disappointed that his first child was a girl. He knew he could never tell anyone that, but that was how he felt. He was into baseball, after all, and knew nothing about dance recitals, Brownies, and Barbie dolls. He comforted himself with the thought that one day, she just might play in the All-State Orchestra—the one dream he had never achieved in his "perfect" life.

Nichole—soon to be known as "Nikki"—was a beautiful baby who became a beautiful child. She engaged her parents, grandparents, and their adult friends as a witty and intelligent girl who was observant beyond her tender years.

But it didn't take long for David and Beth to determine that Nikki would benefit from a sibling. David's practice began to grow, and financially they were in a position to move up to a larger house. They decided the time was right for their second child.

David breathed a silent sigh of relief when ultrasounds revealed that his second child was a boy. Andrew James Heeley was born almost six years to the day after his sister. He was precocious almost from the beginning—a free thinker with a mind of his own. "He's going to be a handful, that one," Nana Dobransky observed, almost prophetically.

Though they hoped for more children, it was not meant to be. Sometimes life throws a curveball.

But for the next seven or eight years, Dr. David Heeley, perfect child, perfect student, and perfect doctor, also saw himself as the perfect father—and especially as the perfect provider. It never even occurred to him that he was ever-increasingly the less-than-perfect husband. He had career ambitions, and no one could stand in the way of them. No one could stand in the way of his "greedy ambitions," either. Day by day, money—and its accumulation—became more and more important to him.

David went back to school and became a Board Certified Cardiothoracic Surgeon, something he wanted to do to increase his income. Of course, this meant even more time away from his wife and kids, but he determined that it would be worth the sacrifice.

Despite the fact that his time was becoming more and more diluted, David Heeley loved his wife and two kids with most of his heart—and all of his wallet. He bought them everything they needed or wanted—all the desires of their hearts. He convinced himself that "things" were a meaningful substitute for time.

Though they were still very young, when he did spend time with Nikki and Andy, David taught them the value of an education, the importance of personal excellence, and the significant roles of proper grammar and impeccable etiquette.

As time went on, he increasingly ignored the lessons his own mom and dad taught him:

"Money isn't everything."

"Spend time with one another."

"Don't miss the games, dance recitals, and concerts."

"Freely demonstrate forgiveness and compassion."

"Go out of your way to take time to communicate."

"Above all, remember that hugs and kisses mean far more than words."

David's actions were based more on selfish desire than on love. His words became increasingly caustic. He openly expressed his disappointment with the performance of his surgical team…as well as with his wife and children.

David's heart had become hard and cold. His wife noticed, and it brought tears to her eyes. His children began to sense that something had changed, and they became fearful of their father. Everyone in his life knew that something was different about David. But David really didn't see what was going on—or how drastically he had changed.

THREE

A Shocking Truth

David James Heeley never imagined that there would come a day when he would watch his almost perfect life completely unravel.

It all began one weekend, when his now 21-year-old daughter, a third-year honor student at Northwestern University, spent a rare weekend at home. Nichole, a diligent student and a leader in her sorority, apparently needed a break from academics and the "party life," even though she was only a few weeks into the fall semester.

Saturday night, as the family sat around the dinner table picking away at what was left of the grilled salmon, David uttered four fateful words to Beth. "It was awfully dry." Beth glanced up at him, the beginning of a tear forming in the corner of her eye. She quickly looked away.

"Can I be excused now?" Andy asked.

"Andrew, you know that is not the way to ask. Try again," David demanded.

"Um...*May* I be excused?"

"Why? You have a bunch of text messages waiting for you?"

"It's the way we talk these days. You guys use the phone. We don't."

Beth interceded. "Yes, Andrew, you may be excused."

"Thanks," Andy said as he bounded up the stairs to his room, eager to leave the unbending rules and sarcastic words of his father behind.

Beth looked at David. The hint of a tear had been replaced by a glare. "Do you always have to be so exacting about every aspect of his language? His clothes? His behavior? He's a teenager. You're a cardiologist, not an English teacher or a prison guard! Most of all, you're a father. Or you should be."

David had his comeback prepared. "Why are you so lenient with him? Why do you cut him so much slack? He needs expectations, or he'll end up working the rest of his life in some dead-end job. Hardly an acceptable life for a doctor's only son."

"He's fifteen. Give him a break," Beth urged.

"See? That's the problem. That's all you do. Give him breaks," the doctor shot back at his wife. "What's wrong with him being a part of the family? Talking after dinner. Telling us what's on his mind. No, instead, he hides in his room, playing stupid video games, texting his buddies, and doing who knows what else. For all we know, the kid could be a pot-head."

"Oh, come on, David! Andy? He's way too sensible for that." Beth was nearly pleading her case—and her son's—to her husband.

Nichole had been silent for most of the dinner. But now, she decided, it was time to speak her mind. She looked her father straight in the eye.

"Dad, you're by far the biggest jerk I've ever known. A massive jerk. I'm sorry, but you are."

David sat stunned as his 21-year-old daughter unleashed her wrath on him.

"It's always about you. It's your way or no way. All you do is demand, demand, demand. That's the way it's been for as long as I can remember."

"That's just your opinion, young lady," he retorted.

"NO, IT'S NOT!" she screamed. "You treat mom like dirt, because she doesn't have an education. Well, maybe that's because she was working so hard to put YOU through medical school. 'Your wife' and I have discussed this, you know. Haven't we, Mom?"

Beth stared at her plate. She said nothing, but, deep down, she was glad this increasingly intense conversation was taking place.

"All I want is for my kids to be achievers. There's nothing wrong with that."

"Andy is 15, Dad. He's a kid. What do you expect him to achieve, anyway? Just because you were a hot-shot athlete and a virtuoso musician and a brainy-brain in junior high and high school doesn't mean *he* has to be. Like Mom says, give him a break. And while you're at it, give me one, too! If you recall, I'm not perfect, either."

"I think I've heard about enough from you for one day!" David's stern tone and piercing eyes suggested that Nichole might want to rein herself in.

"Yeah. Whatever." She turned to her mom. "Mom, I'm going back to the sorority house tonight. I can't stand this."

"Please stay, honey. We're glad to have you home."

Nichole looked at her dad, hoping for some affirming sign. All she got in return was a blank stare that clearly said, "Go." She stood up, brought her dishes to the sink, gathered her belongings from her bedroom, hugged her mom goodbye, and drove off into the night.

David sat at the dining room table the entire time, wondering what had really just happened in his house.

FOUR

Life Minus One

Andy sleepily staggered his way down the stairs earlier than usual Sunday morning. He was ferociously hungry. He needed food more than he needed sleep. Typical teenager!

His mom and dad were in the kitchen, basically ignoring each other. David was reading the sports section of the *Chicago Tribune.* Out of nowhere, he said, "Way too late in the season for the Cubbies to come around."

"Huh?" Beth mumbled in reply.

"Oh, nothing. I don't know why I bother."

Beth didn't know how to take that, so she simply let it go.

"Where's Nikki?" Andy asked. "I want to talk to her about something."

Beth was the one to answer. "She went back to campus."

"Why?" Andy pressed. "I thought she was home for the weekend."

"I thought so, too," his mom replied.

"Things change," his dad added.

"Is there something I'm not getting here? Some hidden clue, or something? Like, why am I always the one who doesn't know what's going on?" Andy asked.

"She said she had things to do. Things she had forgotten about," Beth offered.

David admitted the truth. "No, that's not it! We had a fight. She thinks I'm a big jerk, so she left."

Andy was hesitant at first, but finally he muttered, "Looks like the tuition money for her psychology degree isn't going to waste after all."

If Dr. David Heeley, the leading cardiologist in the Chicago area, had been a violent man, his 15-year-old son would have ended up in a bloody pile on the floor.

Instead, his own heart broke.

Monday morning rolled around way too early for David Heeley. His head hurt. In typical, though infrequent fashion, whenever something unpleasant knocked on life's door, David answered with a bottle of Kentucky bourbon in his hand. Last night had been sufficiently unpleasant, so he and his bottle became instant friends again.

"You were up late," Beth observed knowingly.

"Lots to think about," David mumbled.

"Does 'Jack' help you think?"

"Doesn't hurt. I better get going. I have two plumbing jobs this morning."

"Plumbing job" was David's preferred euphemism for any number of heart procedures—including angiograms, angioplasties, stent placements, and bypass surgery.

David showered, dressed, grabbed half of a bagel and an insulated mug filled with black coffee, and headed out the door.

No words to Beth. No hug. No kiss.

David Heeley had plenty of time to think on the drive to the hospital. There was a long traffic delay caused by what must have been another huge accident on the treacherous stretch of highway that was just ahead.

Am I really the world's biggest jerk? he wondered to himself. *Or is that just the way Nikki sees me? I've given her everything she's ever wanted. What other kid in college has a Mercedes two-door Kompressor? What was up with her big tirade?*

David pulled into his designated parking spot and walked briskly toward the coronary unit. He met with his patient, carefully explained the procedure, then went to scrub. The only other person in the room was his favorite surgical nurse, Eva Gomez. Eva was so thoroughly competent that the fact that she was young, pretty, and personable always slipped by David's radar.

"May I ask you something, Eva?"

"Sure."

"Do you see me as some sort of ogre?"

"I beg your pardon?"

He pressed on. "Do you think I'm a jerk?"

Eva didn't know how to respond. "Is this a trick question?"

"No, I'm serious. And you can be honest. I want to know what you and the others think of me."

Eva's career flashed before her eyes. She wanted to speak her mind, but she knew she had to be diplomatic in her approach.

"We all know you're under a lot of stress. You get all of the most difficult cases. On top of that, you teach. And you travel to a lot of speaking engagements on behalf of the American Heart Association. So I guess we all understand."

"Understand what?" the doctor asked.

"Well, um...we understand why you're so, um, abrasive sometimes...why you get so short with us. We all wish you'd ease off. Reduce your caseload. Fewer surgeries. More time with your family. Or golfing. Or something. Anything."

David said nothing. But her words lodged themselves in his brain.

The procedure completed successfully, David noticed that he was ahead of schedule. He decided to take a short break in the doctor's lounge, and immediately ran into Dr. Albert Chu, one of his long-time associates at Heeley Cardiology, LLP. David always joked that Albert Herbert Chu—A.H. Chu—should have become an allergist. Dr. Chu had heard it dozens of times, but he still laughed politely every time.

"You have a full day, Al?" David asked to get the conversation started.

"Three in a row. All open heart. I should never overbook like that, but some of these people are on the edge. I did an angiogram on a guy yesterday, thinking it would be a stent job, but he was 95% blocked in four arteries, so we popped him open. The guy's lucky to be alive. Only 63, too."

"Good thing you caught it early."

"Yeah, or at least not too late. He tells me he's been in pain for months. Short of breath, too."

David nodded while thinking about how to pose his next

question. "Al, I've noticed that you're really close to the entire team at the office. And everyone on the surgical staff here loves you. I have never felt that. Sometimes I feel as though I'm an outsider in the practice I started almost 23 years ago. Certainly an outsider at the hospital."

"What's your point?" Dr. Chu asked. "Are you expecting me to confirm or deny that? Do you want my opinion?"

"I want you to be honest with me."

"Well, David, your expectations are very high. You expect perfection. Every day. Every week. Every month...yeah, every year."

"In our business, Al, perfection is the only way. Otherwise people die."

"Some of them die anyway," Dr. Chu suggested. "We do what we can. But we're not perfect. We don't have all the answers. And we certainly don't call the shots. Maybe there are forces we can't see, feel, or understand—another dimension we can't comprehend."

"I don't know about that. All I know is that I do my best every day. When someone dies on the operating table, I wonder if I did something horribly wrong."

Dr. Chu carefully considered his next words. "Maybe it's the fact that you continually try for perfection that messes with your mind. When someone in that operating room doesn't perform exactly as you expect—no, *demand*—you tear into them as if they were deliberately trying to destroy your practice...and your life."

That's it. That confirms it, David thought. *I'm a certified jerk.*

FIVE

A Reason for Thanksgiving

Beth Heeley had lived the past couple of months waiting for one key event in her life: Thanksgiving. Although communication with Nikki had been strained and sporadic at best, she was eagerly anticipating her daughter's short trip home from Northwestern for this traditional gathering of family. Her parents were driving in from Reading, Pennsylvania, and David's dad was flying in from Scottsdale, Arizona, where he had a winter residence on a beautiful golf course. How a long-haul, big-rig driver/factory worker had managed to scrape together that kind of money was anyone's guess. A proud, self-sufficient man, he never even asked for his son's help.

I hope nothing happens to spoil it all, she half-thought and half-prayed. At least she took comfort in the fact that her parents and David's dad got along beautifully. Hard-working, patriotic, ex-military types seem to have a certain bond.

Her thoughts were pleasantly interrupted by a cheery "Hi, Mom!" as Nikki let herself into the kitchen through the garage.

"Hi, honey!" Beth responded with a beaming smile.

Nichole put down her bags and her purse, and gave Beth a hug and a kiss on the cheek. "I've missed you," they said in almost perfect unison.

All is as it should be, Beth thought happily.

"Where's Dad?"

Beth panicked. *Oops. I forgot about that.*

"In his study."

Nikki's steps in his direction were initially without much purpose or certainty. But as she got closer to the door, she gained confidence. This was something she knew she had to do.

She knocked on the ornate oak frame of the open door. David looked up and said, "Well, if it isn't my long-lost daughter," in the most sarcastic, biting way he could. Nikki didn't let that stop her. She took a chair directly across from her father.

"Dad, I want to apologize to you. I was wrong. I'm very sorry."

Her dad's puzzled look was not lost on her.

"I'm serious, Dad. I had no right to blow up like I did. And I was wrong to ignore you for the past few weeks. Besides, you're not the biggest jerk I've ever met. You're not a jerk at all."

Without warning, proud Dr. Heeley blurted out words he never thought he would. "You're not the only one who holds the opinion that I'm a jerk, Nikki. I asked my staff in the office and my team at the hospital, and they basically all agree. For a heart doctor, I sure seem to be missing mine."

"I don't believe that's true, Dad. Otherwise I wouldn't have come to you to plead for your forgiveness. I love you, I care about you, and I want to start over with our relationship. Please understand how important this is to me. Please!"

David's hard exterior—and his voice—cracked almost imperceptibly at that moment. "I do, Nikki. I do."

Nikki rose from her chair, stepped up behind her dad, and wrapped her arms around his neck.

David could never have seen this transformation coming at him. It was a complete 180. The perfect example of night turning into day. He was suddenly flooded with a sense of gratitude—of thankfulness—he had not experienced in years.

The family gathered around the festive dinner table: David, Beth, Nichole, Andy, Chuck and Nancy Dobransky, and "Grandpa Gilbert" Heeley.

They began to pass food-laden bowls, plates, and baskets, when Nichole timidly raised her hand and said, "May I make a special request?"

"What is it, honey?" Beth asked.

Nichole was a little hesitant at first. "Well, I know we don't normally do this—in fact, I don't remember ever doing it—but I would like to say grace, or the blessing, or whatever it's called."

Six puzzled people looked at her.

Nana Dobransky finally broke the awkward silence. "I'd like that, Nichole. Your grandpa and I always say grace at home."

"Now hold on a minute," David protested. "This is my home, and we don't practice religion here. Never have, and we're not going to start now. And this 'grace' thing is the most trite form of religious nonsense I've ever heard of."

Try as she did, Beth couldn't keep quiet. "Well, it's my home, too, and I say we let Nikki do this, if this is what she really wants. Is it, Nikki?"

"Yes, Mom."

David realized this was a trivial—and likely short-lived—notion, so there was no real point in fighting it. Besides, he had vowed to himself that he would do his best to avoid being a "jerk" whenever possible.

So Nikki said grace.

"God, you know I don't know very much about you yet, and that's my fault more than anything. But I'm going to learn. So, anyway, please bless this food and our time together as a family. That's all for now."

Grandpa and Grandma Dobransky followed up with a traditional "Amen."

And thus began the first day of the rest of Dr. David Heeley's new, unexpected journey.

David felt some unmet need to be especially antisocial after dinner, so he scurried off to his study to watch NFL football. He didn't even invite the other men to join him.

It was a horribly uneven matchup, and since his beloved Bears weren't playing, he couldn't decide whether to pull for the underdogs, or hope that the better team mercilessly pounded its rival into the turf.

It wasn't long before Nichole appeared at his door. "Is it okay with you if I join you?"

David looked up at her. "Sure, but I thought you didn't like pro football."

"I don't. But I like conversation. And all they're talking about

out there is dessert and leftovers and which Black Friday sales they're going to hit."

David muted the volume on the game and leaned intently toward his daughter. "Talk to me."

Nichole knew exactly what she was there to say. "I'll bet you were kind of surprised by that 'grace' thing at the dinner table."

"Surprised? Everything about you has surprised me since you got home. But I thought you were with me when it comes to all of the intellectual and historical objections to religion, whether it's Islam, Judaism, Christianity, Hinduism, Buddhism, or whatever. They're all the same—captors of the human mind. And the more mindless that mind is, the better it takes hold. I was sure you agreed that it's all gobbledygook. Science proves it. Facts, Nikki. Facts!"

Nichole thought for a minute. "I guess I was with you because you're my dad and you told me that's the way it is. I never really looked at it myself. I never formed my own opinions. I accepted what you told me by faith. And, in many respects, I still agree with your position on religion. Lots of bad stuff happens in the name of God, by whatever name they call him. But, honestly, Dad, I stumbled upon a way of believing that clearly stands out from all the rest. It's based on the life and teachings of Jesus. Pure and simple. Nothing more, nothing less."

"Did you start going to church or something?" David wondered.

Nichole laughed. "No, I started meeting with a small group of people at Coffee Grounds & More, that little restaurant just off campus. People of every imaginable background attend, from a high school student to a professional athlete, to a firefighter, to a banker.

"Sounds boring so far," David observed.

"It's not. Not at all. We eat. We laugh. We even argue. Not everyone is on the same page, and no one even cares. It's just simply an open, honest discussion."

"So does someone lead this discussion?" David wondered.

"Yes. A new friend of mine, Ravi Bhatia."

"Sounds Indian," David, the amazingly astute father suggested.

"He is. He's a grad student in Global Economic Policy. You'd like him!"

"If I could understand him. All of those tech support people in India have such thick accents. Can't understand a thing they're saying."

"Oh, Daddy, please give him a chance," Nikki begged. "I really think you two will get along. He's very informed on lots of topics. Would you like to meet him?"

"Why? Is he on his way over here now?"

"No, of course not. But you could meet him when the next series of classes begins in January," Nichole proposed.

David looked his daughter straight in the eye. "Nikki, I have to be honest with you. I'm not interested. I've looked into all this Jesus Christ stuff before, and it's just not for me. I can't believe in Jesus or some 'god' who would allow thousands of people in Africa to die of AIDS every day. I'm sorry, Nikki…but no."

Nichole tried not to let her disappointment show. "That's okay. I understand, Daddy. I really do."

SIX

A "Winter Break" To Remember

Andy Heeley had spent the last few days in a state of confusion. Out of seemingly nowhere, his sister seemed nicer. His dad seemed nicer. His mom seemed happier. *What's going on here?* he wondered. Nichole was scheduled to come home for two weeks over the holidays, and Andy was actually looking forward to her stay.

The Heeley family had always observed Christmas, but recently, Andy had begun to wonder why. There was no singing of Christmas carols, no candlelight church service, and no mention of the one who was born in a stable 2,000 years ago. In fact, they didn't even call it Christmas. They called it the Holidays…or more recently, "winter break." Maybe his dad was right. Maybe all of the stuff about Jesus—or any other religious leader—is simply a myth. A fairy tale that defies logical explanation.

Still, there were a few holiday traditions that were duly observed in the Heeley household. The big, lavishly decorated tree set up in the living room. The lights dripping from every inch of every tree and shrub in the front yard. The sumptuous feast on Christmas Eve, and the near-duplicate on Christmas Day… followed by days of leftovers. And the best part of all—the extravagant exchange of gifts! Andy especially appreciated presents related to technology and gaming. New games for his up-to-the-minute game console were at the top of his "gotta have" list. A faster laptop might be nice, too!

Over the next several days, Andy's questions would be answered. A "domino effect" was about to take place before his eyes.

Nichole knew there was a good possibility her dad wouldn't like it a bit, but she still decided to go for it. So she called her mom.

"My friend, Ravi, has no family in this country. They're all in India. I was hoping it would be okay with you and Dad if I could invite him to spend Christmas Eve with us."

"It's okay with me," Beth replied. "But I can't speak for your father, and he's at the hospital, so I can't ask him."

"I guess I'll just take my chances. I'm sure if Ravi shows up at the door, Dad won't lock him out."

She guessed correctly. David Heeley had somehow prepared himself to welcome his daughter's guest. He just didn't know it would happen today. Nevertheless, he invited Ravi in, took his coat, and offered him a drink. Nikki beamed!

"So what brought you to Evanston, Mr. Bhatia?" David wanted to know.

"Please call me Ravi. I can tell you this: it wasn't your weather," Ravi answered with a chuckle. "I come from Mumbai, and we never see snow. It wasn't a scholarship, either. My father is funding my education."

"What was it then?"

"I came to study at a fine institution, and I came to learn more about America. My part of India is probably the most Americanized of all regions. We read American books, watch American movies, and copy American culture and traditions. We even celebrate the American version of Christmas, although most of my fellow citizens have no idea who Jesus Christ is."

"You mean who he 'was,'" David hastened to add.

"Respectfully, Dr. Heeley, there is overwhelming evidence that Jesus Christ is as alive today as he was two millennia ago."

Nikki interjected a quiet word of caution. "Ravi, I don't think my dad is ready for your way of thinking just yet."

Ravi glanced in the direction of the very stern-looking father of his friend. "I'm sorry, Doctor, I do not mean to offend."

"That's okay. It seems my daughter may have told you how I feel about religion. I guess you would call me a tough sell. I need facts. Evidence. I don't accept things on whim. Or on faith, either."

"I understand completely," Ravi replied. "My father is a chemist. Everything was cause and effect for him. After all, every chemical reaction or combination can be duplicated on a consistent, repeated basis. He was much like you at one time."

"Why do you say, 'at one time'? Did his thinking change?"

"Oh, yes! Very much so."

The doctor didn't know whether to act bored, get "fidgety," or admit to himself and everyone else that he was actually becoming engaged in this conversation. He got fidgety…and Nichole noticed.

"Dad, do you want to help Mom with the hors d'oeuvres?"

"Does she need help?"

Nikki called out to Beth in the kitchen. "Mom, do you need me or Dad to help with the appetizers?"

"Not really," Beth called back. "I'm almost done. I'll be out there in a few minutes."

As a result of Beth's reply, her husband was stranded in a conversation that was not entirely of his own choosing. Oddly, he soon became glad that he was. He loved debate—even over matters as trivial to him as religion.

Ravi tried to pick up the conversation at a logical place. "Doctor, may I ask you what you personally believe about Jesus? Do you believe he existed?"

"Whether he existed or not, I do know that no intelligent, educated person has ever believed that what he allegedly said about himself was true. After all—if I remember correctly—he claimed to be the only Son of God. How arrogant is that? If there is a god, we are all his sons and daughters."

Ravi thought for a moment. "You are right, he did say words to that effect. He was bold enough to declare, 'I am the way, the truth, and the life. No one comes to the Father except through me.'

"Of course, there are countless people over the centuries who have doubted everything about Jesus, and especially those words. In fact, the academic community often raises valid, thoughtful questions. But there is another significant consideration: to believe in what Jesus Christ taught often means we have to believe less in ourselves and our wisdom and experiences. I've heard the word 'EGO' described as 'Edging God Out.' To place faith in the teachings of

Jesus Christ, we have to deny our ego and accept the fact that we cannot get to God on our own. We have to trust in his Son."

"He's right, Dad," Nikki added. "When I first started studying the many religions of the world, I was looking for an easy path that would make me feel good about my great wisdom and discernment. I could figure this out myself. I could assemble my own special religion. I could believe parts of Hinduism, Buddhism, Islam, New Age, or whatever I wanted. Even Judaism and Christianity. And it would all be good."

"Whatever happened to believing in yourself?" David interjected. "That's what I've taught you and Andrew all your lives. You don't need any god to tell you what to do when you use reason to solve your problems. Brainpower. Logic. You know…?"

Ravi got back into the conversation. "What I've discovered… as did my father before me…is that God is not a celestial vending machine who solves problems at our whim. He is the Creator of the universe and all life in it, and Jesus was sent by him to fulfill a divine purpose."

"It's all a fairy tale," David objected. "There was no God of Creation. There was only the Big Bang—a mass of unknown matter of unknown size and composition that exploded into vast space and became the galaxies, stars, and planets…and continues to expand today. Everyone knows that."

"I'm sure everyone does know about that theory," Ravi agreed. "But note that I said 'theory.' For anyone to acknowledge that event as more than theory, they would have had to witness it. Science is the statement of fact, and facts are based on experimentation and observation. To me, that means that the scientist should be able to repeat the experiment in the presence of other credible witnesses."

"I get your point, Ravi, but no one has observed God, either. No one was there with him from the beginning. So he is simply theory, too."

"Respectfully, Doctor, what's easier to believe in—a mass of unknown matter that pre-existed history, or a God who pre-existed history? Matter could exist...but not God? That's why I believe that God is more than theory. I also believe that Jesus Christ became earth's evidence that God exists, and that Jesus became the path to God. He said, 'I and the Father are one.' He also said, 'If you have seen me, you have seen the Father.' So, in our day, to know Jesus is to know God. He said so himself."

"Okay, that may be your belief, Ravi, but the problem is, I've never actually seen Jesus, either."

"That's true, Doctor. But there were hundreds—in fact, thousands—who heard him teach, witnessed his miracles, and were there when he died. At least five hundred people saw him in the flesh following his resurrection. Some of his followers recorded the events of the time in the Gospels of the Bible. But other writers and witnesses who were not followers of Jesus also support the accuracy of the biblical records. The Jewish historian, Josephus, writing at the time of Christ, is one of them."

At that moment, Beth walked in on what she could tell was an intense conversation. "Are we having fun yet?" she asked as she passed around a large tray of hors d'oeuvres.

"As much fun as one can have while engaged in a discussion about religion," David observed wryly.

"Oh, come on, Dad," Nikki chided. "It hasn't been that bad."

"You're right. I admit I'm actually kind of enjoying it. And by the time I've finished my exercises in logic on Mr. Bhatia, here, I'm sure he'll become a card-carrying atheist...or an agnostic, at least."

"Dad!" Nikki protested.

But Ravi caught the intended humor and laughed. "Doctor, I want you to know that I'm willing to listen to you, and I'll respect your opinions. We Christians don't always get things right, so I, for one, appreciate different points of view—even if we don't always agree."

"Well, I guarantee you we won't agree," David assured Ravi, "because your assertions about Jesus are absolutely preposterous! I'm sorry, but they are."

"Why do you say that, Doctor?"

"First, I doubt that anyone could be so delusional. But if he really said the things you claim, he could have made them up to gain attention. Or perhaps he was simply caught up in the times and the circumstances."

Nikki interrupted before Ravi could speak. "Dad, remember how you used to love to read C. S. Lewis's *The Chronicles of Narnia* to Andy and me when we were young? You especially loved the character of Aslan the Lion. You remember?"

A look of tender reflection filled her dad's face. "Yes, I do. The 'Chronicles' are brilliant."

"Dad...those stories are about God. The Lion is Jesus."

"I never saw them that way. I just thought Lewis was a master in his use of language to paint vivid word pictures and tell compelling stories."

"Here's how I interpret it, Dad. Edmund, one of the four children who discovered the land of Narnia in the wardrobe in their old uncle's house, has betrayed Aslan. The stone table—that huge table in the field that listed the laws of the kingdom—is inscribed with the law that the witch now owns Edmund's soul...unless the betrayal is redeemed with blood. Aslan gives himself up for Edmund, and is bound to the table and killed...a trade that the witch is quite happy to make—to destroy Aslan himself!

"The next day, the children discover that the stone table of the law has been broken, and they watch as Aslan comes back from the dead. The creatures that the witch has turned to stone and held in her courtyard suddenly come to life, too. Through Aslan's death, and resurrection, the law is destroyed, Edmund is redeemed, and the lives of those thought dead are restored.

"I think it's impossible to read the story without seeing the parallels, Dad. Professor Lewis could only have made it stronger if he had Aslan crucified."

"Okay, I see your point, I guess. But why are we talking about Narnia? What does C. S. Lewis have to do with our discussion?"

"You know about his many other books, right, Dad?"

"I know *of* them, but I guess I've never had any interest in actually *reading* them."

"Well, Ravi encouraged me to read some of them. I started with *Mere Christianity.* I discovered that C. S. Lewis was more than a brilliant storyteller and a leading professor at Oxford. He became a very vocal Christian who spent years asking the same questions I've asked. The same questions you're asking now."

David unconsciously leaned forward to listen to his daughter.

"Lewis said this about Jesus—Ravi, please help me if I don't get it exactly right, or at least close. He said, 'There are three logical possibilities. If his claims were untrue, either he knew they were untrue, in which case he was an imposter, and an evil one at that. That's the first possibility. Or he didn't know that this was all in his mind, in which case he was deluded. So the second possibility is that he was a mad man with some form of insanity. The third possibility is that the claims he made were true."

"You got it, Nikki!" Ravi confirmed. "That's really very close. To explain a little further, Lewis made the point that: 'A man who was merely a man and said the sort of things that Jesus said would not be a great moral teacher.' He would—as Nikki said—either be insane, or else he would be the Devil from Hell. 'You must make your choice,' he wrote. So either Jesus was, and is, the Son of God, or else he was insane or evil. But, C. S. Lewis continues, 'let us not come up with any patronizing nonsense about his being a great human teacher. He has not left that open to us. He did not intend to.'"

Nikki quickly added, "Dad, countless people followed Jesus while he was alive, clinging to every word of his teaching. And after he died—and rose again from the dead—belief in him, and the things he said and did, spread throughout the known world. His followers were willing to die for him. They were imprisoned, they were tortured, they were beheaded, they were crucified. Would people in their right mind willingly give themselves up for death if it were all a big lie?"

"The two of you sure have your ducks in a row," David suggested. "It's as if you've been plotting this event for months. 'Let's get good ol' atheist Dr. Heeley to accept religion. If he buys it, anyone will.'"

"That's not true, Dad. There's no plot."

"It's not even a matter of plotting or coercing, or any such thing," Ravi added. "If you don't choose to believe, there's nothing Nikki and I can do about it. It's a personal decision. But it's not just about your head. Faith is mostly a matter of the heart."

David, as puzzled as he had ever been in his life, thought

for a moment before he responded. "So...Ravi...Nikki...what you're saying is that faith is an essential part of this...and to have faith, I have to believe in what Jesus Christ said? In my head and heart?"

They both nodded, and Nikki added, "Sorry, Dad, but I really believe that's the way it is."

"And it's my decision?"

"Yes," they replied in unison.

"Then I may be a skeptic forever. If all of this were real, and it was important, it would make a difference in people's lives. Medicine makes a difference. Surgery makes a difference. Technology makes a difference. Why doesn't faith make a difference? Why doesn't Christianity change things?"

"Oh, but it does," Ravi responded. "It changed me..."

"And it changed me," Nikki quickly added. "I realized for the first time in my life that I was self-centered. It was me, me, me. I realized that I was treating people badly. Dad...think about how I treated you."

All David could do in that moment was listen, think, and fight back tears.

Nikki noticed that her dad's eyes were clouding over, but she didn't bring it up. "Dad, the first thing I needed was God's forgiveness for my stubborn and selfish actions. I need to be forgiven for the way I've treated others. But the big thing for me is that I now know that I will live forever with Jesus. Death will never end my everlasting life. I know you won't believe this, but this has become so important to me that I actually memorized several words from the Bible. Here are some of them: 'I am convinced that neither death nor life, neither angels nor demons, neither the present nor the future, nor any powers, neither height nor depth, nor anything else in all creation, will be able to separate us from the love of God that is in Christ Jesus our Lord.'" (Romans 8:38-39, NIV) That's God's promise, and that's real change. And I believe it with all my heart, mind, and soul!"

"How do you know all this stuff, Nikki? How did you get so indoctrinated?"

"It wasn't a case of indoctrination, Dad. I wasn't brainwashed. I learned these things at the Alpha course…something that millions of people around the world have attended."

David looked intently at Ravi. "So you're not a brainwasher preying on young, impressionable minds?"

"No, sir."

"Dad, I may be young, but I am not all that impressionable. I went into this as an adult…as a total skeptic."

"That's right, Doctor," Ravi confirmed. "Nikki asked all of the same questions you've been asking…and more. Alpha is all about asking questions. Everything is an open debate."

David listened patiently. "Here's a question I haven't asked yet. Why do you call it the Alpha course? Is that significant?"

Ravi's answers were brief and straightforward. "Yes, it is. In the Greek alphabet, Alpha means beginning. Those of us who facilitate the Alpha course—and there are thousands of us around the world—do our best to present the things that Jesus taught. We know that faith changes lives, but that change has to have a beginning."

"Beginning?" David wondered. "Like a do-over? A fresh start?"

"Doctor, you've got it! It is. It means that you turn from disbelief to belief. You accept what Jesus Christ did and said as the truth…as a reasonable response to the questions life sends your way. Not mindlessly, but based on the evidence, and on the impact belief has had on others. We are completely okay with giving everyone the opportunity to discuss, to question, and to challenge."

"So in the Alpha course, do you get to hear other people's spiritual perspectives."

"Yes, we do. After an introductory dinner, we meet once a week for several weeks to openly discuss whether or not there is any validity to Jesus' teaching. During the ten weeks we also have a day or a weekend away to learn who God the Holy Spirit is and how he helps and strengthens us to follow Jesus. Each session starts with a meal together, followed by a talk and then an open discussion where no question is too simple or too hard…where no question is out of place. We discuss exactly the kinds of things we all talked about here tonight. The Alpha course started in a church in London, Great Britain, and was developed by a man named Nicky Gumbel. A graduate of Cambridge and a practicing lawyer, he had been an atheist who was turned off by Christianity because he thought it was boring, untrue, and irrelevant. But after reading the Bible, he discovered that Jesus' teachings made sense, and there was purpose behind Christ's life, death, and resurrection. As a result, the course is built on the basics… the fundamental things that encouraged Nicky Gumbel to take a serious look at what Jesus said—and why countless millions believe his teachings."

"So I take it you personally believe that Christianity is interesting, true, and significant? Or maybe relevant? Is that the word you used?"

"That's exactly it."

"How exactly did you persuade Nikki to believe your way?"

Nikki interrupted. "Dad, that's not what happened at all. This was an open discussion. Ravi facilitated the discussion, but he never asked leading questions nor tried to 'sell' anything."

"That's true, Doctor. At Alpha, we never attempt to force or pressure anyone to believe. That would be dishonest. We simply present the evidence, as we understand it, and let others share their perspectives, and make up their own minds. We use the Alpha course to guide our discussions, simply because the materials explore the vital questions that people today have about God and his plan to free us from our old lives and empower us to live renewed lives."

"I see," David responded, not quite in sync with the idea.

Their intense conversation was interrupted when Andy popped into the room. "When is dinner? I'm hungry!"

Then, he noticed Ravi, and stammered, "Uh…um…"

Nikki made the introductions. "Ravi, this is Andy, my younger brother. Andy, this is Ravi. He's my new Indian friend."

"Wow! Cool! What tribe are you from?"

"Not that kind of Indian…Ravi is from India."

"Aw…you had me, like, going there for a minute."

"Dinner is served," Beth announced in formal British accent, pretending to be a servant in her own household. "Kindly do make note of the place cards on the table which designate the seating arrangement for tonight's epicurean experience."

Everyone laughed—except Andy, who didn't get it. "Why are you talking funny, Mom? And what are place cards?"

With everyone seated, David posed a question unlike any he had asked in his life. "Would you like to say grace before we eat, Nikki?"

Four pairs of eyes stared at him in disbelief.

"What? What is it? Is that so strange? I thought that would be important to her."

Nikki smiled warmly. "It is, Daddy. Thank you for understanding."

"You're my only daughter…" he began, and then his voice trailed off.

"Dear Father in Heaven, thank you for my earthly father, for my mother, for my brother, and for my friend, Ravi. Thank you for sending your Son, Jesus Christ, to set me free from slavery to my own selfish ways. Thank you for your promise to be with me all the days of my life, and for showing me through your word the importance of living for you. Thank you that one day I will actually live with you—forever.

"May your blessings be evident to my family and friends, and may this food strengthen us—me especially—to serve you gladly.

"I ask this in the name of your Son, Jesus. Amen…let it be so."

David was actually wiping his eyes when she finished. With a lump in his throat, he said, "Nik, that was quite a lot different from your prayer at Thanksgiving. I'm beginning to realize that this is very real to you."

"It is, Dad."

"I didn't know you were a slave, Nik," Andy chimed in. "When were you a slave? Like, were you in prison or something? Was this when I was really little? I don't remember it at all."

Laughter filled the room.

"C'mon, you guys. I'm serious."

"No, Andy, I've never been in prison. But there are two kinds of slavery. One kind is physical. That's when you are in bondage to another human being. The other kind of slavery is spiritual. It's the worst kind. But I often think about all the people who were brought from Africa to our country to serve as slaves. Even though they were bound by chains and had no freedom at all, many of them experienced spiritual freedom…and that freedom kept them going during those awful times. They sang songs called Negro Spirituals that talked about the freedom they had in Jesus Christ. Songs like "Ain't That Good News," and "He's Got the Whole World in His Hands."

Andy was frustrated. "I don't get it. I've never heard any of those songs."

"That's okay, Andy. It took me a long time to get it. It's not the songs that are important. It's the idea behind the songs. What Jesus offers is freedom, and hope, and joy, even in the middle of the worst stuff life throws at us. Thankfully, I took the Alpha course, and slowly began to understand the basics of Jesus' teaching."

Ravi smiled at her. "I think you understood very quickly, Nikki."

The tradition with countless families is to open gifts on Christmas morning. The Heeley family, however, has always exchanged gifts on Christmas Eve.

Andy beamed! "This is my favorite part!"

"Please excuse me while I get my backpack," Ravi said as he left the room and headed to the entryway. He returned a few seconds later. "I have something for each of you."

In turn, they passed out their gifts. Ravi gave an assortment of exotic Indian spices to David and Beth. He gave Nikki a beautiful gold cross on an elegant necklace, also made of gold. And he gave Andy a just-released video game.

"Wow! How did you, like, know I wanted this exact game?" Andy asked.

Ravi grinned. "You have a big sister, you know!"

Nikki gingerly touched Ravi's hand. "Thank you so much. It's beautiful! I have something for you, too." She handed Ravi a small package and he opened it immediately.

"Wow! How did you, like, know I wanted this exact book?" Ravi asked, mimicking Andy perfectly.

Her coy reply made everyone laugh. "You have a little sister, you know!"

With presents opened, everyone helped with cleanup. Ravi and Andy carried dishes to the kitchen. Nikki gave them a basic rinse in the sink, and David put them in the dishwasher. Beth packed the leftovers and put them in the fridge so they could be a part of Christmas Day lunch.

Chores done, Ravi said, "I think it's time for me to head back home, but I have sure enjoyed this time with you!"

Surprisingly, Dr. David Heeley was the first to reply. "We've enjoyed having you here, Ravi. I have especially enjoyed it. You are a thought-provoking young man." With that, they shook hands.

Just as the front door was about to close behind Ravi, he turned to David. "I'd really enjoy having you join us at the next Alpha course. It begins the third Friday in January. I think you'd add a lot of meaningful observations to the discussions. With your scientific perspective, you'd be a valuable contributor!"

"I can be a tough audience, as I'm sure you already know. Are you sure you're ready for someone like me?"

Ravi didn't hesitate for a moment. "Absolutely! We love it when people raise honest but difficult questions at Alpha. So bring on your toughest questions and we'll all discuss them!"

In that instant, while one door closed, another door might have opened just a tiny crack.

After Ravi left and everyone else had gone to sleep, Nikki decided she needed to "come down" by watching some television. About an hour later, she switched off the TV and headed up the stairs.

On her way down the long, familiar hallway to her at-home bedroom she heard horribly alarming sounds coming from Andy's bathroom. It sounded a lot like retching...like a kid losing every bit of his dinner in the most awful way imaginable. Then, it suddenly stopped. She knocked softly on the door. "Andy, are you okay?"

There was no answer. She knocked a little louder, then asked again, "Andy, are you okay? What's going on?" Without warning, the awful sounds of liquids and solids spewing into the toilet started again—this time more violently than before. Then, once more, the sounds stopped, and she heard soft moans coming from her brother.

She gingerly tested the door. It seemed to be locked. She wiggled the handle and tried to open the door more purposefully. Definitely locked.

Nikki bolted down the hallway toward her parents' wing of the house. She arrived out of breath and pounded on their door. "Mom! Dad!" she screamed. "Something's wrong with Andy.

He's locked in his bathroom, and it sounds like he's throwing up. And I mean really bad. Like dying, almost!"

Beth and David quickly threw on their robes and followed their daughter down the hall. David hammered his fists on the door while testing the lock. "See if his bedroom door is locked. We'll try to go in the back way."

A weak plea emanated from the bathroom. "No. Please. No. I'm fine."

The protests were too faint and too late. Andy's bedroom door was, in fact, unlocked. David, Beth, and Nikki charged in and entered the bathroom from the inside.

What they saw was both shocking and disgusting. Andy was nearly passed out, half naked, his pajama top in a smelly, soiled pile on the floor. A broken vodka bottle had covered almost every inch of the room with dangerous, sharp-edged shards of glass. Because Nikki was the only one still wearing shoes, only her feet could remain injury-free. She leaned over her brother, who was pale and gaunt.

"Let me, Nikki," David said as he knelt on the slivers of broken glass, cutting painful gashes in his knees. He checked his son's pulse and breathing rate. "Look at me, son. Look me in the eyes," he urged.

Andy complied as best he could, then, almost imperceptibly, said, "I'm sorry, Dad. I'm sorry, Mom. You, too, Nik. I didn't mean for this to happen."

An agitated father responded with the beginnings of what was certain to be a tirade. "Didn't MEAN for it to happen? What on earth were you thinking? You are bombed. Wasted. Plastered. You're lucky we're not calling 9-1-1 right now. Alcohol poisoning is serious stuff. You could be dead, Andrew James."

Beth was sobbing. "Please stop, David. He's been through enough. He needs to get some sleep. Please just clean him up and get him to bed."

"C'mon," David said as he placed his hands under Andy's arms. "Time to get up." The two of them staggered and stumbled back into the bedroom. "You two go to bed. I'm going to stay here with him until I am 100% sure there are no aftereffects."

Nikki wasn't ready to leave. "What can I do, Dad?"

"Nothing, Nikki. You've done your part in simply finding him and alerting us. Just head for bed. Everything will be okay...."

Andrew Heeley experienced a fitful night of sleep. His father tried to get some rest in the overstuffed chair Andy lounged in when he was playing video games online, but sleep eluded him.

At sometime around 8:15 in the morning, they were disturbed by a timid knock at the door. "Anyone awake in there?" It was Beth.

David slowly opened the door, and Beth was shocked by the very first thing she saw. Her husband's knees, shins, and feet were covered with blood.

"You're a doctor! You know better than to leave wounds unattended," she scolded. "You could have bled to death."

"I'm not worried about it," David mumbled in reply. "My blood clots quickly. Almost too quickly. It's thicker than frozen butter."

"Still...."

"Beth, we have a situation here that is far more serious than some minor glass cuts. We have a son who nearly killed himself by alcohol. We need to find out what else is stashed away in his room."

A look of terror covered her face. "Do you think he has pot? Meth? Cocaine?"

"I don't know. But we're going to find out. I'll look on the shelves behind his books. You check his desk and dresser. Then we'll start on the closet."

Semi-consciously overhearing the conversation, Andy struggled to get out of bed. "Dad! Mom! There's nothing else. Only the booze I had last night…and it's gone."

David looked straight at his son. "I don't believe you."

"Dad, it's true. Keep searching around if you don't believe me."

"I think I will…."

After a thorough search turned up nothing, David ordered Andy to sit down. "We still need answers to some questions, young man."

"Yes, sir…."

"Let's start with, where did you get the bottle of vodka?"

"From you."

"From me? I never gave you a drop!"

Andy was terrified to continue, because his secret would be out. But he knew he had no other choice. His dad was on a mission to find answers.

"One night when I was taking out the recyclables, I found one of your empty vodka bottles. After that, every time you drank part of a new bottle, I'd pour some of it in my bottle…a little at a time so you wouldn't notice…until I filled it up. I did the same thing with your whiskey, but I drank that a few nights ago. I also stockpiled one beer out of every 12-pack you brought home."

David was both shocked and angered by this revelation. "Why would you even *think* of doing this?"

"I guess I saw how drinking calmed you down after a day of tough surgeries. I have my own problems every day, you know, so I figured now that I'm, like, an adult—"

David cut off his son in midsentence. "You are not an adult! You are nothing *like* an adult! You are fifteen. You should be drinking Snapple."

Andy sat in front of his dad completely speechless. He instinctively knew that adding any comment right now would be unwise.

"All I can tell you, Andrew, is that things are about to change around here. You can count on it."

During that uncomfortable exchange in Andy's bedroom, neither of them had any idea of the depth and certainty behind those words.

SEVEN

Alpha—from the Beginning!

A few weeks after Christmas, David Heeley drove to the Coffee Grounds & More, and found what he was convinced was the last parking space available. He was not sure he wanted to do this. In reality, he was more certain that he didn't.

"Oh, whatever," he muttered to himself. "I promised Nikki I'd give it a chance for one night."

When he stepped inside, he didn't recognize anyone...not Ravi, and not his daughter. So he asked the long-haired young man behind the espresso machine, "Is there a group called Alpha that meets here?"

"Sure thing. They're in a room over there. It's just past the restrooms. In fact, I'll be joining you as soon as I clock out for the night."

"Thank you," David said, as he headed toward the restrooms. The young man called after him. "You know they serve dinner every week, right? But you have to be here at least half an hour earlier. An hour would be best."

"Thank you," David called back. "I knew that, but things ran late at work." He took a left at the rest rooms, and sure enough, there was an open door that welcomed him into a small, packed room where the remnants of what must have been a dinner featuring Indian food were being cleaned up.

He waved at Ravi, spotted Nikki, and started walking in the direction of the open seat that she had apparently saved for him. On his way, he nearly stumbled over himself when he noticed a woman he knew. It was Eva Gomez, his favorite nurse in the OR.

"What are you doing here?" he whispered to her.

"Same thing you are, I imagine," she whispered back. "Just trying to discover the meaning of life. Get some answers. You know?"

"The truth is, I'm here because my daughter practically begged me. She and her young friend over there."

"Oh, you mean Ravi? He's a wonderful guy…very focused. And he's passionate about his beliefs."

"Trust me. I can tell."

Eva continued. "He's focused on his educational goals, too. He wants to become a cardiologist. You know that, right?"

"You're kidding! He told me he came to the U.S. to study international finance…or something like that."

"Well, that may be why he came, but his new goal is to become a member of your profession."

"No kidding! How do you know this, Eva?"

"I learned about it from Dr. Chu. He's been mentoring Ravi, telling him all about the field…the ups and downs…the stresses…the rewards."

"Chu? Why didn't he tell me? That's kind of sneaky! Wonder what he was—"

Eva interrupted him. "Speaking of Dr. Chu, there he is." She nodded in the doctor's direction as he entered the room. "Since he missed dinner, I didn't expect him to show up."

"Neither did I! But not for that reason."

Albert Chu spotted his two medical associates and headed in their direction. "David, what brings you here? Or should I just assume it was Nikki's doing? I don't recall you having an interest in the teachings of Jesus."

"It was Nikki," the doctor admitted. "But a bigger question is, what are *you* doing here?"

Dr. Chu laughed. "Surprised, huh? I took the Alpha course last fall, at the same time Nikki did. We both had the opportunity to spend some time discovering the amazing things Jesus said and did. It was really enlightening."

"So why are you back now?"

"David, I'm here to learn the things I may have missed last time. The reason is that I'm hoping to volunteer for Alpha in the future. This is part of my preparation."

Dr. Heeley was puzzled. "You're telling me you've accepted all this stuff about Jesus Christ? You follow him now?"

"That's what I'm telling you. When I was a high school student, I was a very ardent follower. I told practically everyone I met about Jesus. Same thing the first three or four years of college. Then, as I approached medical school, my career became too important to me, and it took over. I turned away. I ignored everything I knew. It wasn't until I discovered the Alpha course that it became clear to me that faith is far too important to ignore."

David was about to respond and ask about Ravi's change in career plans when Ravi stepped to the front of the room, got everyone's attention, and introduced himself.

"I'm Ravi Bhatia, and I'm from Mumbai, India. I came to Northwestern to study Global Economic Policy, but since meeting my friends Nichole Heeley, her father, Dr. David Heeley, and his associate, Dr. Albert Chu, I have decided to pursue a career as a medical doctor—a cardiologist." He gestured in David's direction. "Dr. Heeley didn't know this until now, but he had a great influence on my decision. His daughter, who admires him very much, told me about all the wonderful things he's done...how devoted he is to saving lives, even at great personal cost. Then, his associate, Dr. Chu, was kind enough to provide the details about the required education and the expectations of the profession. So my decision was made!"

The group applauded enthusiastically as Ravi continued. "The reason I want to be a cardiologist is because I believe it's important to have a role in repairing damaged hearts and preserving life whenever possible."

There was more applause.

"But even more important is the reason I volunteer to host the Alpha course...the reason I'm here tonight, and for the next nine weeks. We all have a physical heart that beats approximately 100,000 times a day and pumps our blood through our bodies to keep us alive. But I want to investigate with you whether we also have a spiritual heart at the center of our being. In particular, is the Bible telling the truth when it teaches that our spiritual heart is separated from God and needs to be restored into a relationship with him? I suggest that there is some evidence this is true, based on our own selfishness and stubbornness, and the way we often treat others with disrespect or disregard."

David seemed to get lost in these words. *Spiritual heart?* he wondered.

"Before we continue, let's all introduce ourselves to the rest of the group," Ravi suggested. "Tell us your name, what you do, and what brought you here tonight."

Beginning with the young, long-haired barista who had slipped in at the last minute and was leaning against the wall because no seats remained, everyone took thirty seconds or so to tell the group about themselves. In addition to Nikki, Eva, David, and Dr. Chu, there were about 10 to 12 other people, representing the most varied backgrounds that could be imagined.

Among others, there was a campus police officer in his mid-30s, a recently divorced mother of two who was desperately seeking a job, a history professor at Northwestern who appeared to be in his 60s, a junior at Evanston Township High School who was a star wide receiver for the Wildkits varsity football team, and a woman in her 50s who drove long-haul, big rigs for a major trucking company and said she'd have to rearrange her schedule in order to attend future classes. She hoped her employer would cooperate.

David was intrigued by the fact that a woman in the group had the same job as his dad once had. *Small world,* he thought. He also couldn't help but notice the diversity of the group: every race, every generation, every educational background, and every economic status. He was even struck by the sense of humor in the group. The introductions were punctuated with wisecracks and jokes. *This might not turn out to be as stuffy as I imagined it would be.*

After short introductions were completed, Ravi began the class with the basics. "As many of you know, 'Alpha' is the first letter in the Greek alphabet. It literally means 'beginning.' Whether you believe in the Big Bang Theory, or in Creation by a Higher Power, we all realize that the universe had a beginning."

Ravi must really enjoy talking about this topic, David thought to himself.

"I personally believe the teaching of the Bible, as do millions around the world—from the poor to the wealthy, from the illiterate to the highly educated, from the very young to the very old, from every race and nation. I believe that God is the Alpha—the beginning of the universe, and that Jesus Christ is his Son. One of the reasons why so many people from all walks of life have come to this very logical conclusion is that there is overwhelming evidence that can't be ignored."

Evidence? What kind of evidence? David wondered silently.

"Let's start our discussion tonight with a question. Do you believe that the great Greek philosophers such as Aristotle, or Socrates, or Plato, or Euphrates, or Euripides ever existed? Anyone can volunteer."

The history professor raised his hand very politely. "I do, for one," he confirmed.

"Why is that? Why do you, Professor?"

"Because we have their writings. Their own written words and the records of others throughout history confirm their existence, and their impact on the society of their time, as well as on the world of today. After all, Aristotle's *Politics* is one of the greatest governance documents ever written, and his *Poetics* still serves as a clear model for dramatic writers, screenwriters, and playwrights today."

"Okay," Ravi pressed. "How about Julius Caesar or Augustus or Tiberius, or even Nero? How do we know they lived?"

"The historical records, of course. History creates the undisputed trails to the past," the professor replied, as others nodded their heads in agreement.

"Are you ready for an interesting question? If you base your decision…and your beliefs…on the amount of evidence, as well as the dating of that evidence, who *really* walked this earth… Julius Caesar or Jesus Christ?"

The truck-driving lady shouted out, "Jesus Christ, of course! I've never heard anyone at a truck stop yell 'Julius Caesar' when they saw the total on the diesel pump."

Even David Heeley couldn't help but laugh at that one!

Ravi chuckled and continued. "My feeling is that you are far better off believing that Jesus Christ not only existed, but that he actually rose from the dead, than you are to believe that Aristotle or Augustus ever walked the earth.

"Scotland's F.F. Bruce, a noted scholar, historian, and theologian, points out that for Julius Caesar's work, *Gallic War,* the history series of military campaigns written between 58 and 51 B.C., there are only nine or ten copies in existence. The oldest has been dated some nine hundred years later than Caesar's day.

"For Livy's *Roman History,* written between 58 B.C. and 17 A.D. there are no more than twenty copies, the earliest of which also comes from around A.D. 900.

"Of the fourteen books of the histories of Tacitus, only twenty copies survive. Of the sixteen books of his *Annals,* ten portions of his two great historical works depend entirely on two manuscripts, one from the ninth century and one from the eleventh century.

"Yet no classical scholar doubts the authenticity of these works, even though there is a significant time gap, and there are relatively few known manuscripts.

"But when it comes to the New Testament—the account of the life of Jesus and his disciples—we have vast amounts of supporting material. The New Testament was likely written between

A.D. 40 and A.D. 100. There are full manuscripts of the entire New Testament in amazing condition dating from as early as A.D. 350. This is a time span of only 300 years from the time of Christ—a far shorter period than that of the other works I've mentioned. There are papyri containing most of the New Testament writings dating from the third century, and there is even a fragment of John's Gospel dating from about A.D. 130. There are more than 5,000 Greek manuscripts, more than 10,000 Latin manuscripts, along with 9,300 other manuscripts, as well as at least 36,000 references in the writings of the early church fathers. To me, that is evidence that can't be refuted. Over the years, numerous scholars—including many who do not claim to be Christians—have affirmed the validity and accuracy of the Scriptures.

"By the way, this information is included in a book called *Questions of Life* written by Nicky Gumbel, who is behind the development and worldwide growth of the Alpha course."

"So you're saying, 'The older the better?" the divorced mom asked.

"Well, June, what do you think is more believable?" Ravi asked.

"I suppose the manuscripts that were written as close to the actual event as possible," she answered.

"Exactly! But one question people ask is 'How do we know that what they wrote down has not been changed over the years?' This is a great question! But I really believe the answer is that we do know, very accurately, through the science of textual criticism, that today's versions of the Scriptures convey the same ideas, words, and events that the New Testament writers wrote about. Essentially, the more texts there are, the less doubt there is about the original. As Professor F. F. Bruce demonstrated in his book, *Are The New Testament Documents Reliable?*, the New Testament is a manuscript that can clearly be supported by comparing the biblical texts with those of other historical works.

"What's important in all of this is the picture of Jesus Christ that emerges. So, I now want us to consider the person, Jesus Christ," Ravi suggested. "Are you all okay with that?"

"That's why I'm here," Josh, the high school student, called out. "Sorry, but I don't even like Indian food."

Everyone laughed…including Ravi.

Ravi continued. "One of the fascinating things about Jesus is that so much of his teaching was centered on himself. He said to people, in effect, 'If you want to have a relationship with God, you need to come to me.' He claimed, 'I am the way, and the truth, and the life. No one comes to the Father except though me.' (John 14:6, NIV) It's through a relationship with Jesus that we encounter God. Furthermore, it is clear from what he said and taught that Jesus was claiming to be God himself. However, just because he claimed this doesn't mean he was correct. He could have been deluded or insane or he could have been evil by trying to deceive people. The third logical option is that he was correct.

"To honestly investigate which option is most likely, we can look at five bits of evidence and, against each one, we can ask the question, 'Does this best fit with someone who is insane, evil, or actually God?'

"The first piece of evidence is his moral teaching. Although we have advanced in many areas over the last two thousand years, no one has come up with a better set of moral values than Jesus Christ. Things such as 'love your neighbor as yourself.' Is this most likely to have come from someone who is insane or evil? Or could it have come from God?

"The second piece of evidence revolves around his character. The historic records show that people loved him—especially little children and the downtrodden and outcasts.

"Third, the miracles he performed—and these were also recorded by other historians at the time.

"The next piece of evidence involves the 300 or so prophecies written hundreds of years before he came to earth—as recorded in the Old Testament. These include where he would be born and where he would be buried.

"The fifth and last piece of evidence we're going to discuss is the evidence of his resurrection from the dead. Having clearly died on the cross, he was seen by over 500 people over the next six-week period.

"Putting this evidence together, we are faced with the fact that Jesus was neither insane nor evil, but rather, he was and is God. As C. S. Lewis put it, 'Amazing as it may seem, God had actually visited planet earth.'"

After Ravi finished presenting the first talk on "Who Is Jesus?" it was time for open discussion. This was the part of the evening that David had really been looking forward to. He wanted an opportunity to express his opinions and to ask some really difficult questions. And he was interested to hear what other people had to say.

Ravi explained, "I'm simply here as a facilitator and I want all of you, as a group, to discuss the evidence that I have presented." He started by posing a question, "What do you think about the idea that Jesus is fully man and fully God?"

The history professor caught Ravi's attention. "I have no idea. But what difference does that really make? How does it affect us?"

"I'm glad you asked that question. It really is the key question that can focus our discussion. Does anyone have any thoughts on that?"

Nikki was the one to respond. "If the records of the life and teachings of Jesus Christ are accurate and complete, as a lot of people believe they are, then nothing can be more important than learning about him."

"Why is that?" the professor wanted to know.

"Because it's difficult to ignore the words of someone who claimed to be God," Nikki answered.

David was pleased to join the discussion and asked, "But what about all the other religions? What about the teachings of Buddhism, Hinduism, Islam, and the teachings of the Dali Lama. Why shouldn't they all lead to God?"

"I'm wondering that, too," said the long-haired barista. "That is one thing I don't like about you Christians. You are so dogmatic. You insist that Jesus is the only way. Like the doctor said, what about the millions of people who follow other religions?"

David was enjoying this. He thought the young barista had Ravi against the ropes. And yet he was surprised that Ravi was not trying to defend what he had said. He respected everyone's opinions and appeared to be enjoying the open discussion.

A new dimension was added to the mix when the long-distance truck driver pitched in with her thoughts, "Actually, I believe we have all originated from aliens and they are watching us from outer space. In fact, I think they may be on earth now, possibly disguised as humans or even animals."

The group was quiet for a moment and then Ravi responded, "What an interesting point of view, Dee! What do the rest of you think?"

Dr. Chu spoke up. "My understanding is that Jesus' claims to be God are unique and that no other religious leader ever claimed to be God. They claim to be 'prophets,' or 'enlightened,' but they don't claim to be the 'only way.'"

David politely offered his objection. "But Dr. Chu, wouldn't you agree that they all had profound thoughts and taught amazing lessons? That their teachings were meaningful and significant?"

"Oh, most certainly!"

"I thought so."

"On the other hand, Charles Dickens had great teachings in *A Christmas Carol.* William Shakespeare and F. Scott Fitzgerald offered some amazing life lessons. Harvey Mackay, John Maxwell, Pope John Paul II, and Rick Warren have all written books that impact lives in positive ways. But not one of them has claimed to be the only path to God, even though many of them may point you in God's direction."

"True," David admitted. "True."

This lively discussion continued for nearly forty minutes. Then sensing the time, Ravi glanced at his watch. "Unfortunately, we're out of time tonight. I promised you we wouldn't run over on time, and I'm going to stick to that. But I hope to see you all next week, same time, same place. For those of you who arrived late, you missed my best recipe from Mumbai—if you like curry!"

Everyone cheered and shouted, "It was great!" Except for Josh. And David, of course, who regretted missing dinner.

Mental note, he thought. Make it in time for dinner next week.

David walked Nikki to her car, gave her a hug, then drove off into the night, his mind filled with questions. He had really enjoyed the open discussion and the opportunity for everyone to speak their mind without feeling awkward or being embarrassed. *But do I believe what I heard tonight?* he wondered.

EIGHT

More Questions than Answers

"Are you planning to attend Alpha tonight?" David asked Albert Chu.

"I sure am. And I plan to be there in time for dinner, too."

"Great, Al! Want to ride together so we're sure to get a parking space?"

"Sounds good to me."

When Drs. David and Albert walked into the back room at Coffee Grounds & More, David sniffed the air, hoping for the exotic scents of Indian spices—especially curry. Instead, the room smelled like barbecue.

They both spotted Ravi and approached him. "Are you serving one of your marvelous Indian specialties tonight?" David asked.

"Nope. Sorry. Tonight is good ol' southern barbecue with corn on the cob. And next week is a Vietnamese specialty, prepared and served by Kim."

"Kim?"

"Yes, Kim Nguyen. She was my fellow student in Global Economic Policy…until I decided to pursue medical school, of course. She attended the last session. Nikki knows her."

"As do I," Dr. Chu added. "Trust me, you'll love her cooking."

The ribs were delicious, although David felt that he had consumed enough fat to increase his "bad" cholesterol well beyond acceptable levels. He was just finishing off a small slice of apple pie when Ravi walked to the front of the room to begin the discussion.

"Welcome, everyone. Tonight, we're going to focus on the all-important topic, 'Why Did Jesus Die?'" He looked around the room. "Anyone have any thoughts on this?"

Mr. High School Football Star spoke up. "Because God told him he had to? Like, it was his job?"

"You've been reading ahead, right, Josh?" Ravi joked.

"No, honest. I haven't," Josh responded timidly. "Um…you haven't given us anything to read."

Ravi laughed. "I know that, Josh. I was just so impressed with your answer. You are right on!"

"Seriously? I was just guessing," Josh admitted.

"Seriously, Josh. God sent Jesus to take our place…to take our punishment for sin. It really *was* the assignment that God gave to his Son. But to take our sins on himself and defeat death through his death, and resurrection, Jesus had to be a pure sacrifice—a substitute for us. God enabled him to be given birth by a woman who was a virgin named Mary. He was a pure sacrifice in our place.

Dee, the truck driver, offered her insight. "That's the Christmas story, right?"

"Right, Dee," Ravi confirmed.

Chuck the cop had a burning question, and raised his hand to ask it.

"Yes, Chuck?"

"Okay, Ravi, it's about this sin thing. I arrest people all the time who are worse off than most so-called sinners. I mean, I arrest fraternity boys almost every night. They are bombed out of their minds. Way over the legal limit."

"Well. Chuck, I believe people like this are chasing after the things they don't need, and turning their backs on the things they really do need."

"Like what?" Chuck asked.

"Sometimes people say, 'I have no need for Christianity.' They say things like, 'I am really basically happy. My life is full and I try to be nice to other people and lead a good life.' In order to understand why Jesus died we have to go back and look at the greatest problem that confronts every person."

Jack in the back of the room shouted out, "I know what it is, Ravi. Credit cards!"

"Close, Jack!" Ravi replied as laughter filled the room. "But if we are honest, we would all have to admit that we do things that we know are wrong. The wrong things we do are called 'sin.' Now, I admit that sin is an old word that hardly anyone ever uses anymore. We all think we are basically good, so how could we sin? Of course, if we compare ourselves to armed robbers or serial killers or even our neighbors, we may think we look good. But when we compare ourselves to Jesus Christ, we see how far short we fall. Somerset Maugham once said, 'If I wrote down every thought I have ever thought and every deed I have ever done, men would call me a monster of depravity.'

"But sin means so much more than robbery or rape or murder. Sin really means rebellion against God. We ignore God as if he doesn't really exist. And worse still, we never thank him or praise him for life, for creation, and for all the good things he has given us. The result is that we are cut off from him. Like the prodigal son you can read about in the Gospel of Luke, chapter 15, we find ourselves far from our Father's home—and we suffer because of this. Sometimes people ask, 'If we are all in the same situation, that means no one is better or worse than anyone else. So does it really matter?' The answer is that it does matter because of the consequences of sin in our lives, which can be summarized under four headings."

Uh, oh! Here we go. I'm guessing I'll nod off during this talk, David thought.

Ravi continued: "The first is 'the pollution of sin.'

"Jesus said, 'It's what comes out of a person that pollutes: obscenities, lusts, thefts, murders, adulteries, greed, depravity, deceptive dealings, carousing, mean looks, slander, arrogance, foolishness—all these are vomit from the heart. There is the source of your pollution.' (Mark 7:20-23, The Message)

"Right now, you may be thinking, 'I don't do most of these things.' But doing one of them—and only one—is enough to mess up our lives. We might wish the Ten Commandments were like a test paper in which we only have to score seven out of ten. But the New Testament says 'Whoever keeps the whole law and yet stumbles at just one point is guilty of breaking all of it.' (James 2:10, NIV) It is not possible, for example, to have a 'reasonably clean driving record.' Either it is clean or it is not. One driving offense stops it from being a clean record. So it is in our relationship with God. One offense makes our lives unclean."

David glanced in Eva's direction and mouthed the words, "Yada, Yada, Yada."

"Shhhh!" Eva mouthed back.

Ravi had much more to offer. "The second consequence of sin is 'the power of sin.'

"The things we do wrong have an addictive power. Jesus said, 'Everyone who sins is a slave to sin.' (John 8:34, NIV) It is easier to see this in some areas of our wrongdoing than in others. For example, it is well known that if someone has taken a hard drug like heroin, it usually becomes an addiction.

It is also possible to be addicted to bad temper, envy, arrogance, pride, selfishness, slander, or sexual immorality. We can become addicted to patterns of thought or behavior that, on our own, we cannot break. This is the slavery that Jesus spoke about, and it has a destructive power in our lives.

Carol, a very trim fitness instructor, stood up and raised her hand. "Ravi, I'm addicted to exercise and a vegan diet. Does that make me a hopeless sinner?"

Over the chuckles, Ravi suggested, "No, Carol, that just makes you healthy…unless you're not getting your protein."

"Oh, but I am!"

"Good! We wouldn't want you to waste away! Okay, everyone, the third consequence of sin is 'the penalty for sin.'

"Something within each of us cries out for justice. When we hear of a child being molested, or an elderly person attacked in his or her home, or a baby who is shaken or battered, or people cheated out of their life savings by unscrupulous 'investment counselors,' we all hope that the people who have done these things will be caught and punished. Our motives may be mixed; there may be an element of revenge. But there is also such a thing as justifiable anger. We are correct in our feelings that sins should be punished; that people who do such things should not get away with them.

"The personal problem for us is, it is not just other people's sins that deserve punishment. It is our own, as well. Sooner or later we'll all have to face God, regardless of our condition. 'We will appear before Christ and take what's coming to us as a result of our actions, either good or bad.' (2 Corinthians 5:10, The Message)

"The fourth consequence of sin is 'the partition of sin.'

"We all know that we are going to experience physical death someday. Many of us have witnessed death first-hand…and it's usually not a pretty thing. Am I right, Dr. Heeley? Am I right, Dr. Chu? Am I right, Ms. Gomez?"

All three of them nodded in agreement.

Ravi continued: "As bad as physical death is, it is spiritual death that leads to eternal isolation from God. This cutting off from God begins now. The things we do wrong today cause a barrier that, unless dealt with, will separate us from God for all eternity.

"Here's a fact. We all have a need to deal with the problem of sin in our own lives. The greater our understanding of our need, the more we will appreciate what God has done. Because he loves each one of us so much, he sent his only Son, Jesus Christ, from heaven to earth to show us what he is like and to deal with the problem of sin.

"God, in Jesus Christ, became our substitute. He took our place. We all rebelled against God, living selfish lives and causing pollution from the sins we commit. But in his mercy, Jesus represented each one of us on the cross when he took the punishment we all deserve. One day, I believe we will realize the damage our sins have caused and, according to God's fair and just judgment, that we deserve death. However there is good news because Jesus Christ took the punishment on himself when he was crucified. Now it's up to us, individually, to decide what we're going to do about his offer of forgiveness and a relationship through the sacrifice of Jesus Christ. He has promised to help us heal our relationships with others. He has promised to forgive us for our missteps. He has promised everlasting life."

The discussion was even more interesting that night, but David was gripped by the closing questions that Ravi put to the group. "How do you feel about Jesus being your substitute on the cross?" he asked, as he looked around the room and glanced into every pair of eyes. "And, my friends, what are you going to do about that?"

At that moment in Coffee Grounds & More on that winter night in Evanston, Illinois, Dr. David Heeley didn't have an answer to those questions. He wasn't sure he ever would.

NINE

The Next Steps for Everyone!

On the way from her last class to her sorority house, Nikki made what would turn out to be a very important call. "Are you going to be home for dinner tonight, Dad?"

"Yes, I am, Nikki. I'm on the road now. Should be home in about twenty minutes."

"Do you mind if I join you all for dinner?"

"You know I'd love that!"

"And Mom is okay with a last-minute guest?"

"Of course," David Heeley reassured his daughter. "She's your mom."

"I know...but she's seemed kind of distant from me since I invited Jesus Christ to change my life. She won't even go to Alpha with us."

David didn't know how to respond. After an uncomfortable pause, he finally said, "I'm only there because of you and Ravi, honey. I'm afraid I am still puzzled by the whole thing. I don't know what to make of it all."

"I know, Dad. And that's okay. But you need to know that the only reason I encouraged you to attend is because I really want to spend eternity with both of you."

With that, Nikki said, "I'll see you soon, Dad." And she ended the call.

And, with that, David got another tear in his eye—something that had happened quite infrequently...until recently.

"Did you know that Nikki's on her way?" David asked his wife. "She wants to have dinner with us. Hope you're okay with that."

"Of course I am," Beth responded. "I haven't seen her since you two started this Alpha thing. In fact, I haven't seen her since winter break. I talk to her on the phone, of course...." Her voice trailed off unexpectedly.

"Andrew," she called loudly, "please come down here and help set the table."

He called back, "Be right there." And, sure enough, he was.

Moments later, Nikki walked in through the entrance from the garage to the kitchen, hugged her mom and dad, then walked over to Andy and said, "Brother!"

"Sister!" he responded.

Beth was taken aback. "Okay, what's this all about? What are you two up to?"

"Nothing," Andy replied.

"We'll tell you at dinner," Nikki added coyly.

"I'm sure you would like to say grace, Nik," David suggested when they were all seated at the dinner table. "In fact, I'm getting used to it."

"Not tonight, Dad."

David couldn't believe it. "What?"

"*I* want to say grace," Andy said meekly.

"What?" Beth wondered aloud.

"You tell 'em, Nikki. Okay?" Andy needed his sister's support for this one.

"Mom, Dad," Nikki began. "I took some time recently to tell Andy about Jesus Christ and how deeply he is loved by his savior. And he invited Jesus Christ into his life."

"You're kidding, right?" David and Beth asked in practically the exact same words at exactly the same moment.

"No, Mom. No, Dad," Andy assured them. "I began to realize all the things I've done wrong…and all the ways I've hurt people…especially my family."

"Oh, Andrew, you've always been a good kid. We love you. Don't we, David?"

"Yes, we do. Sometimes, I just don't realize how much I really love you."

"Like when I stole your booze and got blasted out of my mind?"

"I wasn't going to bring that up, Andrew."

"But you could if you wanted to. The thing is, Dad, that was the old Andrew Heeley. I am all new now. All forgiven. And I haven't swiped your alcohol or had a drink since Christmas break. I swear."

"Believe him, Dad," Nikki added hastily.

"I do."

"And you, Mom?"

"I do, too."

With that, Beth began to pass a bowl of salad and a huge platter of baked mostaccioli around the table.

Before Andy loaded his plate with his favorite Italian dish, he said, "Remember, Mom…Dad…I want to say grace."

As all at the table reverently bowed their heads, Andy began a simple but humbling prayer.

"Dear God, I really don't know how to do this, but I guess I'm willing to try. If I remember something I read the other day, when Jesus taught people how to pray, he said we should first praise you, then ask you to take charge of our lives, then ask you to feed us. I guess next, you wanted us to forgive other people, because you have forgiven us. And I know that you want to keep temptations away from us and keep us from doing the wrong things. I know I mighta done this out of order, but my sister, Nik, says what's important is what's in my heart. Oh, one more thing. I want you to be the one who super powers my life, and I want to give you all the thanks for that. So, that's all from me, Andy, the new guy on your team."

"Who *IS* this kid?" David asked aloud…though not intending to do so.

"He's your son, Dad," Nikki answered.

Beth simply marveled at the entire event. Her daughter had changed. Her son had changed. Her husband even seemed like a new David Heeley. What, in God's name, would be next?

TEN

The Decision

Dr. David Heeley walked into the third Alpha meeting at Coffee Grounds & More with just one question on his mind. He approached Ravi immediately.

"May I speak with you after this session is concluded?" he asked with typical grammatical correctness.

"Of course! I always have time for Nichole's father," Ravi beamed.

Kim's Vietnamese dinner was wonderful! Everyone the doctor talked to agreed that they had enjoyed flavors they had seldom—if ever—experienced before.

The time seemed to race by, even though the session ran almost ten minutes over. David waited patiently while several other people approached Ravi, asked him questions, thanked him, and said their goodbyes. A tap on his shoulder interrupted his thoughts. "Dad, are you ready to go? I'll walk with you to the parking lot."

"That's okay, Nik. I asked Ravi if I could visit with him for a bit.

Do you want to stay for our discussion? I'm sure you'd add a lot."

"I'm sorry, Dad. I promised a couple of classmates I'd meet them in the library. In fact, I'm late. I have to run."

In a way, David was relieved to hear those words. He wasn't really sure he was ready for Nikki to be part of the pending conversation. So he hugged his daughter, turned around—and there was Ravi, with that ever-present grin on his face.

"Doctor, you wanted to talk with me?"

"Yes I do, Ravi. Thank you for taking the time. I know it's getting late."

There was an unusually long period of silence as David groped for the right words.

"Yes?" Ravi encouraged.

"Well, I'm just wondering...how do you do it?"

"I'm sorry, I don't understand. Do what?"

"How does someone have a relationship with God...with Jesus? Do you simply say you believe, and the relationship begins?"

Ravi had a quick answer...one that he knew would require a lot more explanation. "That's essentially it. There's a book in the Bible written by a man named Paul that claims, 'If you confess with your mouth, "Jesus is Lord," and believe in your heart that God raised him from the dead, you will be saved.'" (Romans 10:9; NIV)

David was quick to object. "See, that's what you religious people do. You throw some out-of-context words at us and expect us to understand. I've heard the phrase 'You are SAVED!' in movies and on TV...you know, evangelists and such. But what does 'saved' really mean? Saved from what?"

Ravi laughed. "You warned me that you'd be a real challenge, and you are!"

"So that means I win?" a grinning David Heeley joked.

"Not so fast, Doctor! I have an answer!

"Okay, I'm listening."

Ravi eagerly began. "The same biblical writer I mentioned—Paul—in the same book—Romans—taught this: 'All have sinned and fall short of the glory of God.' (Romans 3:23, NIV) 'Fall short' means to miss the target. And the reason every one of us misses the target is because of sin."

David objected. "I know you've talked about sin in the last few sessions, but sin is such an outdated notion. No one believes in the 'original sin' concept, or whatever you call it. I believe that mankind is basically good, decent, and noble."

"Really?"

"Yes, really."

"Allow me to ask you a few quick questions, Dr. Heeley."

"You're on."

Ravi shot one question after another at the doctor.

"Do you ever check a $100 bill…or a $20…to make sure it's real?"

"Do you have locks on your house? On your car?"

"Do you have an alarm system for your house?"

"Do you ever struggle to open a CD or DVD because of all the wrapping and security tape?"

"Do you ever consider the possibility that a drunk driver just might cross the center line and kill you and everyone in your car?"

"Do you ever worry about Nikki walking across campus alone at night?"

"Do you personally know people who have cheated on their spouses?"

In every case, David answered, "Yes, Yes, Yes, Yes, Yes, Yes, Yes."

"The reason you answered 'Yes' to all of those questions is because you actually already believe that all have sinned."

"I believe that 'some' have sinned—or are capable of sinning. I've never committed any of the sins you've suggested. I may drink, but I've never driven drunk. I've never stolen. I've never raped anyone. I've never cheated on Nikki's mother. In fact, I am 100% truthful when tax time rolls around. I don't even cheat the U.S. Treasury. Not one dime."

Ravi responded, "That's commendable. But let's look at the less visible sins. Anger. Jealousy. Greed. Pride. Lust. Even rejecting a relationship with God is a form of sin, because he created us to know and worship him.'"

"Okay, I guess I'd have to admit to anger, and maybe some of the others."

Ravi's next statement shocked the doctor. "And, based on that admission, you deserve the death penalty."

"WHAT? How can any of those things lead to the death penalty?"

"My friend, I'm not talking about physical death. That's universal, as you well know. Eventually, we will all face it. No, I'm about talking spiritual death. That means eternal separation from God and his love."

"Why would God condemn anyone to that? God is supposed to be love, after all. That's what all you people preach."

Ravi had been asked that question before, so the answer was well formed in his mind. "God is not the one who makes the decision. We decide on our own. To quote Paul, Jesus' follower, again, 'The wages of sin is death, but the gift of God is eternal life through Jesus Christ our Lord.' (Romans 6:23, NIV) So God has created an 'out.' An escape hatch. He has offered us life through his Son. It's our choice: death or life. Faith in Jesus Christ is what 'saves' us from spiritual death."

"It all sounds so morbid," the doctor observed, "death, eternal separation from God."

"I'm sorry, but I see it as a beautiful plan. A plan that leads to eternity with him. It's a plan that's hopeful…it's filled with promises…and it's evidence of God's love."

"Good luck explaining that one, Ravi."

"Doctor, have you ever noticed those signs in the end zones at football games? The ones that say 'John 3:16?'"

"Of course. They're obnoxious. Why would a football fan display a sign like that? It's obviously about some Bible verse."

"It is. But fans display them because they are fans of God and his love. And they care enough about you to try to share that message with you."

"Seems like an odd way to go about doing that. I don't even know what the reference is. I just see 'John 3:16.' I don't know what it says."

"Well, you've come to the right place!" Ravi said as both men chuckled. "It says, 'This is how much God loved the world: He gave his Son, his one and only Son. And this is why: so that no one need be destroyed; by believing in him, anyone can have a whole and lasting life.'" (John 3:16, The Message)

"I'm beginning to understand what you're saying," David finally admitted. "But I still don't know what the next step is. This all goes back to my first question. How do you do this?"

"I know you're going to think that I spend my entire life quoting from Paul's letter to the Romans, but you asked, so here goes: 'If you confess with your mouth, "Jesus is Lord," and believe in your heart that God raised him from the dead, you will be saved. For it is with your heart that you believe and are justified, and it is with your mouth that you confess and are saved.'" (Romans 10:9-10, NIV)

David was still puzzled. "What does 'confess with your mouth' mean?"

"Doctor, what do you do when you perform a successful surgery and you have good news for the patient?"

"I tell them the good news right after the effects of the anesthetic wear off, of course. I want them to know."

"That's the way it is with the good news of God's love for us. We want people to know. That's why I volunteer for the Alpha class. That's why Nikki is becoming increasingly bold about telling others what she's discovered. That's why fans display 'John 3:16' banners at sports events. It's not just about our life here on earth…it's about eternal life."

"Ravi," David said softly, "I'm ready to believe in my heart. I'm ready to confess with my mouth that Jesus is Lord. *My* Lord."

Like every other human being, David Heeley had made tens of thousands of decisions in his life. Some were trivial…such as what kind of toothpaste to buy, or what TV show to watch at the end of a grueling day. Some were merely small…what kind of car to drive. After all, does it really matter, as long as it runs and can dependably get its owner from point A to point B safely?

But other decisions were giants in his path…beginning with the decision to attend Cornell, followed by his decision to marry Beth, his decision to attend medical school at Johns Hopkins and become a cardiologist, and then a cardiothoracic surgeon, heading up his own thriving practice. In fact, every day he was faced with making critical choices with his patients that could result in life or death. These may be the most difficult decisions anyone could ever confront.

In his daily life apart from work, some of David's decisions were based on convenience. Others were based on opportunity. Some were based on desire, and still others on need—real or merely perceived.

Then there were the unconscious slights and oversights. Years of unwarranted mental, emotional, and spiritual disconnect from his wife. Years of "too much going on right now" to give his children the attentive fathering they craved…and needed.

But on this cold February night in Evanston, Illinois, David was prepared in every way to make what could easily be the most significant decision of his life.

This decision would demand that a rational, thinking, highly educated doctor tie up his doubts, objections, and disbelief into a neat little package and dispose of it. This was the day when a figure from history would be invited to enter his earthly life and usher his soul into eternal life—beginning at this moment in time and lasting forever. This was the day when David Heeley, MD, would become David Heeley, Man of Faith and Child of God.

Ravi led David through a simple, straightforward prayer. He asked for forgiveness, he agreed in his mind and heart that Jesus was Lord, and he accepted God's love for him.

He knew his faith was at the "Alpha" stage—at the very beginning—but he knew that he had a good friend in Ravi, who immediately suggested that he should join a local church where other Christ-followers would help and guide him in this new journey of faith.

Ravi left David with a parting thought that frigid winter night—a verse from one of the Apostle Paul's two personal letters to the Christians in Corinth: "Therefore, if anyone is in Christ, he is a new creation; the old has gone, the new has come!" (2 Corinthians 5:17, NIV)

As David Heeley drove home that night, he felt as though he had just inhaled the biggest gulp of fresh air he ever had in his life. He felt clean. He felt forgiven. He felt that he was free of the proverbial 500-pound gorilla that had been clinging to his back. He felt brand new!

ELEVEN

A Storm on the Radar

"You're really late tonight," Beth observed as David walked in after his Alpha meeting. "Later than usual, anyway. Did you go out for dessert with Nikki?"

"No, I stayed to talk to Ravi."

"That doesn't sound like you at all."

"Well, Beth, it was like me tonight. I needed to get some answers."

"Did you get them?"

"Yes, I did. At least I think I did. I think I've put my faith in Christ. In fact, I know I have."

Beth was incredulous. "You mean you're 'saved'? As in 'Hallelujah, praise Jesus?'"

"Yeah, that's basically it, Beth. Although those are not the exact words I'd use. I'd say maybe, 'My faith came alive.' "

"C'mon, David! You've got to be kidding!"

"In a way, I wish I were. But in other ways, I'm glad I'm not."

"Okay, I'm stumped," Beth admitted. "I know Nikki and Andy

think they somehow became disciples of Jesus. But you? You're going to have to explain."

"I know we haven't talked about spiritual things much throughout our marriage," David began. "In fact, you know that I never wanted to talk about that. Then Nikki came home one weekend, and she was a whole new Nikki. Next, along comes Ravi, and the things he says start making sense. So, why not give Alpha a try? Something different. Something out of the ordinary."

"I know. I was here through all of this," Beth said.

"Yes. Yes, Beth, you were. But you weren't at Alpha. And it's my fault that I didn't tell you more about this, so that Nikki, or Andy, or me putting our faith in Christ didn't come as such a huge shock to you."

Beth looked at her husband without speaking, as if she were silently encouraging him to tell her everything. David understood her cue and continued, adding as much detail as he thought he should.

"Beth, there was this follower of the teachings of Jesus, known today as the Apostle Paul—"

She interrupted. "Even though I became disillusioned about the whole idea of faith and Christianity after high school, I went to Sunday religious education as a kid, you know. And I remember. Paul was the guy who was persecuting and killing Christians until a big event—blindness or something—resulted in a huge change. He became a follower of Christ and wrote several books in the Bible. And he ended up in prison because of his beliefs."

"That's the guy," David agreed, thinking to himself that this story would now be much easier to tell. He reached into his vest pocket for a small New Testament of the Bible that Beth didn't even know he owned. "In one of the letters Paul wrote, he explained the Christian faith very clearly."

David eventually found the right page and read, "'…it is by grace you have been saved, through faith—and this is not from yourselves, it is the gift of God—not by works, so that no one can boast.'" (Ephesians 2:8-9, NIV)

"What exactly does that mean to you?" Beth wondered. "Are those words the reason you think you are saved—or whatever you call it?"

"They're not the reason, exactly. They're the explanation of how it happens."

"I'm listening…."

David continued, enthusiasm building in his voice. "I learned that there are four key words in that single sentence: Grace, Faith, Gift, and Works.

"Here's what Ravi told me those words mean. Grace is 'unmerited favor.' Grace is what God offers to us, even though we don't really deserve it.

"But we have to personally receive God's Grace, God's forgiveness, and God's favor…by faith. I've always rejected the notion of faith, until Ravi described it as 'the substance of things hoped for, the evidence of things not seen.' (Hebrews 11:1, KJV)

"You know how important physical evidence is to me. I believe it's as important in medicine as it is in law. But, as Ravi pointed out, I never witnessed the 'Big Bang,' nor did I witness Creation, so I decided it's as rational to believe in one as to believe in the other. Ravi also asked me to evaluate the evidence for the existence of Christ, the certainty of his death, and the probability of his resurrection. The evidence is clear! So even though I never witnessed any of this, I have accepted it by faith."

By the nodding of her head, and by the fact that Beth had leaned forward in her chair to the point where she might fall off the edge and land on the floor, David could tell she was interested.

"The third word is 'Gift.' I remember when I was a kid, I'd want a certain thing for my birthday or for Christmas. One year I wanted a microscope. So I asked my parents for it, but I didn't know if I'd receive it. I didn't know if I deserved it. But when I asked God to save me, by his grace, through faith, I knew he'd give me the gift of eternal life, even if I didn't deserve it. That's the nature of grace."

Beth interrupted him. "David, this is getting way too deep for me. I need to go to bed. I need sleep."

"Okay, I understand. May I just explain what the fourth word means to Ravi…and now to me?"

"As long as it's a short explanation…."

"The word 'Works,' as it is used in the phrase, 'not by works, so that no one can boast,' means that there is nothing we can personally do—and brag about—that can save us. That does not diminish the importance of works—of doing good things for God and others. The Bible says, 'Faith without works is useless.' (James 2:20, NASB)

"When I understood the meaning of these four words, I began to understand why Jesus Christ came to earth to die for you and me. Does this make any sense at all?"

"Honestly, David, I have to admit that not much of anything makes sense to me at all anymore. I still have no idea if Andy is drinking or doing drugs, even though he says he isn't. I have no idea what you and Nikki and Ravi are discussing when you have one of your weekly meetings. Sometimes I'm not even sure I still have a husband. I've wondered that for years."

With those words, David stood up, walked over to his wife, and wrapped his arms around her.

"I know you must have thought that...wondered that...more than once. I know that's my fault. All that has mattered to me is building my practice and making more money. I hope I can convince you that I know I was wrong and that, with God's help, I will change. I truly want you to know that I love you. Thank you for listening and understanding, Honey Babe."

Beth's eyes misted over. "David...you...you haven't called me that in years!"

David Heeley had driven the same route to his office and the hospital for years—in fact, every day since the highway first opened. He could almost navigate the trip in his sleep, but this day he paid extra attention to what he was doing. A severe winter storm had slammed the entire Chicago area. The blinding snow and icy road conditions had forced school closings. Even the government had shut down all but the most essential of services.

But hearts still needed healing, and delays could be deadly. Storm or not, David had a full schedule of procedures that day.

"People simply do not use their heads in these conditions," he muttered to himself as he watched car after car after truck pass him, their drivers apparently oblivious to the icy roads. Still, his own speed inched up, minute by minute. *I have a full schedule today*, he reminded himself.

Increasingly concerned about both the time and the road conditions that seemed to deteriorate with each mile he covered, David reached down to his center console to punch the button for NOAA weather reports.

He remembers nothing after that.

Airlifting David's mangled body from the scene of the accident was impossible due to near zero visibility. All helicopters—and even commercial flights out of O'Hare—were grounded. Instead, two ambulances and a fire truck inched their way down the freeway toward the scene, fighting to stay on the road.

Upon her first glimpse of David, a paramedic in the first ambulance said, "Looks really bad. I don't know if we can get him to the hospital in time. Northwestern is the closest, right?"

"Right," said the second paramedic. "I'll tell you one thing... this stretch of road is deadly in good weather. Why anyone would drive it in a storm like this is a complete mystery. I'd take the side streets."

The medics placed David's crushed body on a gurney, lifted him into the ambulance, hooked him up to monitors, and pumped oxygen into his lungs. Then they searched through his pockets to find his I.D. "Hey, this is Dr. Heeley," one of them said.

"Do you know him?" the other asked.

"Yeah, I do. He's the reason my dad is still alive."

"Wow."

"Wow is right." Then, impatiently, she yelled at the driver. "Allan, he's secured! Get this thing rolling! This guy doesn't have all day!"

The ER team let out a collective gasp when they saw who their new patient was. They surged into action, cutting off his clothing while rushing him to a private treatment area. A swarm of doctors and nurses performed immediate examinations.

David Heeley was completely unconscious. His heartbeat and

blood pressure were erratic. His breathing was labored, despite forced oxygen. A ventilator might be the next necessary solution. The medical team worked frantically to address his exterior wounds, while scans and X-rays failed to deliver any clear evidence of the nature of his internal injuries. The only thing they knew for certain was that his head had experienced acute blunt trauma, his rib cage had several fractures, his right hand was severely mangled, and his entire wrist was shattered beyond reasonable hope of restoration.

The speed and intensity of the treatment were astounding. How could something good ever come out of such apparent chaos?

Then someone on the team finally shouted over the din. "Has anyone called his family?"

Beth Heeley was staring out the kitchen window at the blowing and drifting snow, sipping on black coffee, when the ring of the phone snapped her back into the present.

"Heeley residence, Beth speaking," she answered in the formal manner that had been the family's established practice for years. Seconds later, she screamed, "OH, NO! NO, GOD, PLEASE NO!"

The voice on the other end responded, "I'm sorry, Mrs. Heeley. We're doing everything we can. Do you have a way to get here? Is there someone who can drive you?"

"No," she said initially. Then she quickly remembered that Nikki was home on break. "I mean, yes. Yes, I do. I'll be there as quickly as possible."

Beth ran up the stairs toward Nikki's room, pounding on

Andy's door on the way. "Get up, both of you! There's an emergency! Dad's been in a terrible accident. We're going to the hospital. No showers. No breakfast. Move it!"

They got in the car, Nikki behind the wheel. "I hate driving in this weather, Mom."

"I'll drive," newly licensed Andy volunteered.

"Not today," Beth responded. "You've never driven on snow and ice before. It's a lot to handle."

"Even for me," Nikki said as she slowly backed out of the garage.

~

Beth and her two terrified children were shocked into silence at their first glimpse of David. He was connected to nearly every machine and monitor known to medical science. His head was bandaged, but traces of blood had soaked to the surface.

They asked questions of the doctors and nurses in the ER.

"How bad is he?"

"Will he make it?"

"What can we do? Do we need to give blood?"

There were no clear next steps. So they simply waited. And waited longer.

~

It was four days before David's family and friends had any answers.

Both Ravi and Dr. Albert Chu stopped by the ER waiting room several times over those days to try to comfort Beth, Nikki, and Andy. Because he was not family, Ravi was not allowed into David's room, even though the family requested it. But as a doctor, Dr. Chu was.

One day, when he was leaning over David's bed—with Beth and Nikki looking on and listening—Dr. Chu softly offered a prayer on his associate's behalf.

"Dear Father in Heaven…your new follower…your new child… David Heeley, needs your healing touch right now. You have promised in your Word that the plans you have for him are plans for good. Only you know what his life holds in the future. Only you know what wonderful things he will do for you and for others…if you restore him to health. In your name, I ask that you do exactly that! Amen."

Nikki echoed Dr. Chu's "Amen." Beth simply sat in her bedside chair in disbelief. In anger, she asked, "How can you expect me or anyone else to believe in your God? Shouldn't my husband be rewarded for putting his faith in Christ…for following Jesus? Instead, he's being punished. That's wrong. That's cruel. That's sadistic."

Beth's daughter was about to prove that she was wise beyond her years, and knew so much about her new faith.

"Mom," she said, "God isn't punishing Dad. That's not the way God does things. The truth is, we live in an imperfect world. It was made imperfect by our own sin, and that imperfection is why bad things happen. But there's a promise in the Bible that gives us hope for a bright future."

Nikki turned to Ravi. "Didn't you tell me that the Bible says that things that look bad can turn out good?"

Ravi smiled. "That's basically it. The words are, 'We know that in all things God works for the good of those who love him, who have been called according to his purpose.'" (Romans 8:28; NIV)

"I don't understand," Beth admitted.

Dr. Chu jumped into the conversation. "I believe that God is assuring us that even things that are dreadfully bad at the moment can somehow turn into unexpected miracles...and our part is simply to do his will."

"I'm sorry, I *still* don't understand," Beth said with a look of sadness on her face.

Nikki took her mother's hand. "Our prayer—Dad's, Ravi's, Dr. Chu's, and mine...and even Andy's—is that someday you *will* understand."

In the coming days, another very special prayer was answered.

David came out of his deep coma. He began to move. He asked for food. He even cracked a smile and reached out for his wife's and his kids' hands.

Was this the first day of an unexpected miracle?

TWELVE

Another 180-Degree Turn

Ninety-five percent of David Heeley's body recovered fully after his horrific accident. But five percent did not. And that five percent was essential if he planned to continue his career as a cardiothoracic surgeon.

A surgeon with mangled hands and a fractured, motion-limited wrist could never help another patient. Never save another life.

David Heeley, though, was not a quitter. He did everything possible to recover from his debilitating injuries.

But the rehab center and physical therapists didn't help. Massage therapy didn't help. Even self-taught, research-based exercise didn't help.

What helped were his daughter, Nikki, and her friend, Ravi, who had come to visit him at home.

One evening, still in great pain, David asked, "Why would God allow something so awful to happen to me? Why would he take my career...my prized profession...away from me? After all, I believed what the two of you told me about Jesus Christ.

And I believed what he said about himself, even though he said it two thousand years ago. Why?"

Ravi's first thought was, *Now would be a good time to give up! I don't have the answers. I should simply walk out of here right now.* Then he thought, *But I have to try. God, please help me!*

He began slowly, as he thought carefully about every word he was about to speak.

"Dr. Heeley, from your birth, no one in this world could promise you a perfect life. Not your parents, not your baseball coaches or college professors, not your wife, not Nikki or Andy, and not your co-workers in your clinic or in the hospital. Not even God…not on this earth, anyway."

"But I never expected this," David protested. "If God supposedly knows everything, why would he create me, knowing this would happen?"

"Doctor, God created you to live with him. Earth is just a short stop on the way to eternity. Earth tests us, heaven is our reward, based solely on a genuine faith in Christ. Also, we will receive rewards in heaven for how we live our lives for him here on earth. If God had said, 'All of life will be perfect for you, if you simply believe in me,' there would be no doubters. If that were true, who wouldn't believe?"

David's anger began to surface. "That's rubbish, Ravi. I know life isn't perfect, but I was helping people. I was saving lives. There are hundreds of people walking around today because I fixed them with the skill of my hands. Now my hands are worthless. Why would God test me in such a cruel way?"

"You've already written the end of your life story, then," Ravi suggested, rather than actually asking. "You already know what

God has planned for the rest of your days. You don't believe that miracles can actually happen."

"Miracles? Where was God in all this? Why would my skill be taken from me? Why should I count on a miracle to bring it back?"

"Doctor, I hesitate to tell you this, but you were not injured because of God. The roads were icy. The snow was blinding. Your car did not have enough traction. You slammed into the back of a slow-moving snowplow. God did not tell you to get in your car that day. God did not tell you to take the most accident-prone freeway in Illinois. God did not tell you to drive in those conditions."

David was not at all happy with Ravi's stern approach to his questions. "I'm amazed you don't have some Bible verse that covers this," he suggested sarcastically.

Nikki glanced at Ravi for his confirmation before she reached into her purse for a small Bible, so she could take on her dad's question herself. "There is, Dad. We learned it at Alpha. In the Gospel of John, Jesus is quoted as saying, '…in me you may have peace. In this world you will have trouble. But take heart! I have overcome the world.' (John 16:33, NIV) In a letter written by John, he says, 'Who is it that overcomes the world? Only he who believes that Jesus is the Son of God.'" (1 John 5:5, NIV)

"I haven't overcome anything…."

"Oh, but you have, Daddy! You're a new person! Like the Bible says, 'Old things have passed away.' You have eternal life in your future. God IS paying attention to you! There is something deeper going on here than any of us understand. Your life is changing, but it may not be changing in the way you want or expect."

"She's right, Doctor," Ravi added. "Remember the verse I shared with you the night you prayed to invite Christ into your life? 'If anyone is in Christ, he is a new creation; the old has gone, the new has come!'" (2 Corinthians 5:17, NIV)

"Okay…okay, Ravi. I think I knew what it meant THEN, but I really don't know what it means NOW."

"Doctor, I hope you know that I hurt deeply as I watch you go through all of this crushing pain. I know that it would be unbearable if God hadn't made promises that he will never break. One of those promises is: 'God's Spirit touches our spirits and confirms who we really are. We know who he is, and we know who we are: Father and children. And we know we are going to get what's coming to us—an unbelievable inheritance! We go through exactly what Christ goes through. If we go through the hard times with him, then we're certainly going to go through the good times with him!'" (Romans 8:16-18, The Message)

"What does that mean?"

"It means that life is more than temporary. It means that it is eternal."

David Heeley spent the next several weeks walking around his house and yard, often thinking and planning, occasionally praying, and sometimes even cursing. He knew the cursing was somehow wrong, but at times he couldn't help himself.

With no income from surgical procedures that he could personally perform, he had to find creative ways to keep his clinic afloat. Without a clear plan, he knew he might have to downsize his practice, maybe sell the family's home, and move into something more affordable. Over time, he became more comfortable with that idea. *At least I'm alive*, he thought as he thanked God for each new day.

But despite his growing faith, his prayers, the prayers of his family and friends, and the support of the staff at his clinic and at Northwestern Hospital, Dr. David Heeley, Chicago's leading cardiologist and cardiothoracic surgeon, never performed another life-saving surgery. However, over time, he did begin to suspect that maybe God was going to use the accident to birth a new and exciting chapter in his life!

The team at his clinic continued the work of saving lives. David appointed Dr. Albert H. Chu as head of staff...a good decision! Eva Gomez left the hospital staff to become an integral part of the Heeley Clinic team. And, as you might have already guessed, Ravi Bhatia was accepted to medical school, and worked very hard. Over time, he became filled with knowledge, filled with passion, filled with compassion. And increasingly filled with the love of Jesus Christ.

Almost three years to the day after his accident—as his family and Ravi gathered around the dinner table—David said, "I don't like to make a big deal out of this, but it *IS* my turn to ask for God's blessing." They all agreed, and so he began...

"My dear loving Father in heaven. Thank you for this new and amazing relationship I have with you through Jesus Christ. Also, thank you for enabling me to see and enjoy life from another dimension. I so appreciate the love, peace and joy you have given me through the work of the Holy Spirit in my life, and for giving me eternal values that have replaced my own selfish earthly values. Thank you for blessing us again with the food before us. Thank you for Al and Eva and everyone at the clinic.

Thank you for my beloved wife, Beth, and for her budding faith in you. Thank you for my son, Andy. Thank you for Nikki, who cared about me, prayed for me, and introduced me to you through Alpha. And, finally, Lord God, thank you for Ravi, that special guy with tons of faith and plenty of curry powder. Help him to understand that he would be a welcome addition to our family…and that it just might be time for him to propose…."

"Daddy!"

"David!"

"Really, Dad! Like, get real! Not your job, dude!"

EPILOGUE

A Last Word from the Author

I'm guessing that many of you may have lots of questions rushing around in your minds—and hearts—right now.

Some of you may be wondering if this is a true story. Is there really a doctor in Evanston, Illinois, named David James Heeley? Does he have a wife named Beth, and two children, Nikki and Andy? Did he really get in a horrible accident? Did his newfound relationship with Jesus Christ impact his life and empower him to conquer seemingly insurmountable obstacles? And, finally, is there really something called "Alpha" that can help you understand who Jesus Christ is, and why he is relevant today?

Some quick answers.

There really is an Evanston, Illinois.

There is no real David Heeley…or Elizabeth Heeley…or Nichole Heeley…or Andrew Heeley. But there are millions like them…millions who live lives of frantic, uncertain desperation.

There is no Ravi Bhatia, but there are real men and women of every race, every nation, and every economic status, who love

God and share his message with passion.

There are people the world over whose lives are affected by tragedy...by accidents, by illness, by death. But God offers everyone an answer...and peace of mind and heart...through Jesus Christ.

True, this story, despite its tragedy, has a happy ending. But not all such stories do. Not on earth, at least. But in eternity, YES!

So, dear reader, how do you find out more? This book is not in your hands by accident right now. You are reading this page because someone—a friend, an associate, a coworker, a spouse, parent, or child—cares about you, loves you, and wants you to know and understand the truths that have impacted their lives.

That brings us to our final question: Is there really something called "Alpha" that can help you understand who Jesus Christ is, and whether he is relevant today?

The answer is "yes." Alpha courses include a meal together followed by a talk, either live or using a DVD, and then an opportunity for discussion in small groups. For the sake of the story, we combined the talk with the sort of questions that come up in the discussion groups. The latter are very open, providing an opportunity for people to ask any question they want on the topic of the talk or anything else such as, "Why is there suffering in the world?" and "What about other religions?"

The course includes a day or weekend away to understand who God the Holy Spirit is and what he does to help us to be a Christ-follower. Alpha courses are offered in thousands of locations the world over. You can go to our website, ***www.alpha.org*** to find a course location in your area. All courses are free, and you are not asked to sign any kind of agreement or pledge.

The Alpha courses offered near you will cover many important topics that were not discussed in this book.

Here are some of them:

- **Why and How Do I Pray?**
- **Why and How Should I Read the Bible?**
- **How Does God Guide Us?**
- **Who Is the Holy Spirit?**
- **What Does the Holy Spirit Do?**
- **How Can I Be Filled with the Spirit?**
- **How Can I Resist Evil?**
- **Why and How Should I Tell Others?**
- **Does God Heal Today?**
- **What About the Church?**
- **How Can I Make the Most of the Rest of My Life?**

The Alpha course is not affiliated with any denomination and is currently being offered by thousands of Protestant, Catholic, and Orthodox churches. But you don't need to belong to any of those traditions! You may be Buddhist or a Muslim or a Hindu or from any of the world's other religions, or you may be agnostic or an atheist. Classes are open to, and attended by, people of all backgrounds, ages, and beliefs. (You can find endorsements on our website that indicate the diverse appeal of the course.)

For the purpose of the story, we have taken some liberties about how the Alpha course works. Discussions can and often do go off in very interesting directions. Deep issues and questions of life that people simply do not often have the chance to raise are discussed. At Alpha, all opinions and points-of-view are welcomed and respected. There are no wrong ideas, no out-of-place suggestions. In a very real way, all participants are respected as individuals… and for their opinions. This is all about exploring life's questions and challenges in an open and honest way. And YOU are invited to be a part of it!

Not everyone that attends an Alpha course decides to become a Christian and follow Jesus. In fact, I have received letters from people in groups that I have personally hosted, thanking me for the course and for opening their minds to Jesus' teaching, but telling me that Christianity was not for them. That is their decision and I am not going to chase them down to convince them otherwise.

However, if you do have questions about the meaning of life, please consider joining the millions of people across the world who have attended an Alpha course to investigate the teachings of Jesus. The claims he makes about our eternal destiny are incredible and, at the very least, it is worth investing ten weeks to consider whether they are true. As I once heard a past guest who came to faith in Jesus in an Alpha course say that, when inviting friends, he offers a challenge: "What have you got to lose by attending an Alpha course, but more importantly, what might you have to gain?" What might YOU have to gain?

For more information, to find a course near you, or to speak to someone, visit ***www.alpha.org***.

Please share your personal experience with this book with us at ***www.alpha.org***. In the U.S. only, visit ***www.alphausa.org/mystory***.

RESOURCES

Recommended Reading

Alpha - Questions of Life

This book tackles some of the key questions people face when giving consideration to the claims of Christianity. Written with honesty and common sense, the book points the way to an authentic faith that is exciting and relevant to today's world. Topics include: Who is Jesus? How can we have faith? and, How can I make the most of the rest of my life?

The God Who Changes Lives

In their own compelling words, a wide variety of people tell the stories of their lives and how they have been transformed—often in dramatic circumstances— through an encounter with God. Some have been healed, some powerfully changed, and others given the strength to face troubled times.

30 Days - A Practical Introduction to Reading The Bible

Invest 30 days in exploring the Bible by reading one key biblical passage each day. *30 Days* includes a portion of Scripture, a challenging commentary, and suggested prayer for each day of the month. An excellent tool for those who are beginning to explore the Bible.

Why Jesus?

A thought-provoking booklet designed to drive to the heart of the claims of Christianity; also available in a 20 minute DVD presentation.

A Life Worth Living

In the future, scientists will be able to prolong life, but will it be worth living? Without purpose or joy, extended life seems a hollow victory. So how do we, in fact, live life to the fullest? *A Life Worth Living*, based on Paul's letter to the Philippians, is a practical and positive guide to achieving exactly this, uncovering in us a new heart, new purpose, new attitude, and a new confidence to the way we live our lives.

Searching Issues

Searching Issues tackles seven of the most difficult and complex questions surrounding Christianity in an honest and straightforward manner. Questions covered include: Why Does God Allow Suffering? What About Other Religions? Is There Anything Wrong with Sex Before Marriage? What is the Christian Attitude to Homosexuality? Is There a Conflict Between Science and Christianity?

These and other titles can be found at ***www.alpha.org*** or 1-800-DO-ALPHA (U.S. only).

RECOMMENDED BIBLES

There are several excellent translations and paraphrases on the Bible that are available online, at major general bookstores, and at Christian bookstores.

Here are two we especially recommend:

The New International Version (NIV)

Copyrighted by the International Bible Society, and published by the Zondervan Corporation, Grand Rapids, MI.

THE MESSAGE: The Bible in Contemporary Language, by Eugene Peterson

Copyrighted by Eugene H. Peterson, and published by NavPress Publishing Group, Colorado Springs, CO.

Other excellent versions of the Bible include:

- **The New American Standard Bible (NASB)**
- **New Jerusalem Bible (NJB)**
- **St. Joseph New American Bible, The Catholic Study Bible**
- **The New Living Translation (NLT)**
- **The New King James Version (NKJV)**
- **The Revised Standard Version (RSV)**

ACKNOWLEDGEMENTS

This book would not have come to be without the support and encouragement of many special people in my life.

My beautiful, loving, caring wife of 29 years, Jeannie, who will always dance before my eyes as she did as a professional ballet dancer when we first met. Anyone who really knows her loves her, but none more than I do.

My now-adult children, Rebecca and Ben, are amazing! Rebecca, who is a wonderful support, a champion and a rare jewel for Jeannie and me. Ben, who is a friend as well as a son—someone with an outstanding heart of love and kindness toward people.

My other beloved son, Alex, who, in a cloud of confusion, made a terrible decision and left us far too early. He is now home with his heavenly father—long before any of us would have chosen. I always believed all of my children would outlive me. That's every parent's hope, yet it was not to be. But sadly—and maybe even thankfully—I am not in charge.

My Dad, who showed me what love looks like and went to be with the Lord without warning; my Mum, who is a true disciple of Jesus Christ—an inspiration and a champion through the valley of the shadow of death. My big sister, Jax, who always loved and cared for me and who suffered so much and finally finished her race and went home so quickly. My big brother, Kim, always so close and able to laugh with me, and my dear brother, Will, with whom I've journeyed through affliction, sharing brotherly love in the flesh and the spirit. Will recently lost his battle with cancer and went to heaven—and I miss him dearly.

My team at Alpha USA is Amazing in every way! My outstanding assistant Janelle who keeps her smile and efficiency through the pressure, and all my friends and fellow workers in the harvest field including our Board of Directors, Central Support Team, Regional Directors, and National Coordinators. Special thanks, too, to all our Alpha practitioners and volunteers, who spare so much of their time to see the lives of others impacted.

There are many people to thank for their role in helping to make this book a reality. First, to my new friend Ken Blanchard who originally suggested this book and has encouraged me every step of the way. We are going to do a sequel together highlighting Ken's ministry, Lead Like Jesus. Since its founding in 1999, this very timely organization has become a movement that is finding a home in places as diverse as primary schools and prisons, credit unions and congregations. Transcending cultures, languages, economics, and geography, Lead Like Jesus is transforming leaders into servant leaders of true greatness, like Jesus modeled for us. Ken has long been personally acquainted with the Alpha course and how it can inspire people to serve a greater cause, because he has taken the course himself. And because the Alpha course and Lead Like Jesus work so beautifully together to build faith and empower individuals to live life in a way that carries a bigger impact, several people on the Alpha staff, as well as a number who have completed the Alpha course, have enrolled in Lead Like Jesus encounters.

To Steve Gottry, who was magnificent in putting all the words together especially after recently undergoing an emergency quadruple heart bypass. Steve, it's been a privilege and a blessing to work with you.

I also want to thank Robert and Eric Wolgemuth who have been wonderful consultants in this project and a great source of encouragement and friendship.

And to Mike Singh, who has done a fantastic job in coordinating so much of THE BREAKTHROUGH, thank you for all your encouragement and support with the initiative. Mike, you're a star.

Finally, I want to thank and acknowledge Steve Gottry's team who helped complete the book: Dave Gjerness, who designed the book cover and helped with "research on the fly"; Eric Walljasper, the designer of the interior pages; Steve's daughter, Kalla Paige Gottry, who did transcriptions; and his proofreading team, including Dave Gjerness, Linda Purdy, and Virginia Van Der Geest.

My dear readers, my hope is that you will discover one small nugget of truth in this book...one glittering reality...that will transform some aspect of your life. A small thing. A big thing. A past healing. A future event. Or maybe even the keys to a breakthrough life far beyond anything you ever imagined or expected!

ABOUT THE AUTHOR

Gerard Long

Executive Director, Alpha USA

Following a dramatic encounter with God in 1980, Gerard has lived with one burning ambition—to please the Lord Jesus and to obey His will. He had been planning to build on his success as a runner and businessman, but, after his encounter with God, he felt a calling to serve in a church in North London. He was at this church for 22 years, including 17 as a pastor, while also working in the banking and finance industry.

Gerard has a BSc (Hons) Banking and Finance degree and worked for HSBC (one of the largest banks in the world) for 30 years, retiring at the end of 2006 as a senior vice president. His banking career took him around the world and included some fascinating roles including Director of the Year 2000 Program (Millennium Bug) for the UK and Europe. In 2002 he moved to New York to launch a global product and then moved to Chicago to direct the integration of HSBC and Household Finance, following the latter's $13.8 billion purchase in 2003.

He has appeared on TV and was quoted in major newspapers both as an advisor on the Millennium Bug (Y2K) and as a Christian living for Jesus Christ in the city of London. All through his banking career, Gerard sought to introduce his colleagues to Christ and led many Alpha courses in the workplace. Prior to moving to the US, he was also Chairman of Christians in Finance (founded in 1875).

As well as experiencing wonderful joy in knowing and serving the Lord Jesus, Gerard has known the deepest grief and suffering in the loss of his youngest son. This, and a number of other painful trials, has served to heighten Gerard's desire to complete the work that God has for him and, in particular, to see as many people as possible come into a personal relationship with Jesus Christ.

In 2006, Gerard decided to leave behind a lucrative banking career and join Alpha USA. He now leads the organization whose mission is to serve local churches in presenting the good news of Jesus Christ through the Alpha course. He has witnessed many incredible conversions to Christ merging faith and work for nearly three decades—including running Alpha in the Workplace in boardrooms across two continents, as well as at home, in churches, jails, and clubs. (Alpha is now being run in over 169 countries, and more than 15 million people have gone through the course). Because Gerard is passionate about the ministry of Alpha, he has donated all of his potential royalties and income from this book, now and in the future, directly to Alpha North America. He will not personally profit in any way from the release, distribution, or sale of this book.

Gerard lives with his beautiful wife, Jeannie, in Lake Forest, IL. His daughter, Rebecca, also works for Alpha USA, and his son, Ben, works in London. To relax, he enjoys spending time with family and friends, his two golden retrievers, golf, skiing, tennis and gardening.